THE COSTS OF PRIVACY

SOCIAL INSTITUTIONS AND SOCIAL CHANGE

An Aldine de Gruyter Series of Texts and Monographs

EDITED BY

Michael Useem • James D. Wright

THE COSTS OF PRIVACY
Surveillance and Reputation in America

Steven L. Nock

ALDINE DE GRUYTER
New York

ABOUT THE AUTHOR

Steven L. Nock is Associate Professor of Sociology at the University of Virginia. His research focuses on the dynamic role of the family in responding to and transmitting social changes. He is author of *The Sociology of the Family,* co-author (with Paul Kingston) of *The Sociology of Public Issues,* and co-editor (with Peter Rossi) of *Measuring Social Judgements.* His most recent research deals with the role of the family in structuring and transmitting obligations across and within generations.

ALDINE DE GRUYTER
A division of Walter de Gruyter, Inc.
200 Saw Mill River Road
Hawthorne, New York 10532

This publication is printed on acid-free paper ⊗

Library of Congress Cataloging-in-Publication Data

Nock, Steven L.
 The costs of privacy : surveillance and reputation in America / Steven L. Nock.
  p. cm.
 Includes biographical references (p.   ) and index.
 ISBN 0-202-30454-X (cloth : acid-free paper). — ISBN 0-202-30455-8 (paper : acid-free paper)
  1. Privacy, Right of—United States. 2. Records—United States--Access control. 3. Reputation (Law)—United States.
 4. Confidence. 5. Trust (Psychology) I. Title.
 JC596.2.U5N63 1993
 323.44′8′0973—dc20   92-35480
                                                            CIP

Manufactured in the United States of America

10 9 8 7 6 5 4 3 2 1

CONTENTS

5. CONCLUSION

PREFACE

Several years ago, a very bright student of mine was interviewed for an entry-level position with a bank in Washington, D.C. While discussing the interview with me, she casually mentioned that she had been asked to submit to a drug test. This required that she be accompanied to a bathroom where she provided a urine sample to her monitor. At that time, drug tests were not that common and I asked her if it bothered her. Her reply was the impetus for this book. She told me that she did not mind the drug test because she did not use drugs. It was that simple for her. There were no larger issues involved. I was surprised that such a talented young woman would be so nonchalant about something that would have troubled me greatly. I was also surprised that she did not see such a request as an invasion of her privacy. Indeed, she saw the drug test as routine and unexceptional.

It was soon after that I began to study privacy as a social and legal concept. It became clear that the meaning of this concept has changed greatly over time. Indeed, there was little discussion of it 200 years ago. Concerns related to personal privacy, I discovered, are more typical of modern-day American society than of Colonial or early-American times. The social history of that era suggests that privacy as we *now* understand it was less important and less widespread. If personal privacy is defined as the legitimate denial of access to, or scrutiny of, one's behaviors, then it is clear that we enjoy more privacy today than did our ancestors. One does not need to romanticize the past to appreciate the extent to which many things now viewed as legitimately private were once subject to much greater exposure. The structure of earlier communities and dwellings, the central role of the church, and the greater reliance on informal methods of social control contributed to more routine observation of others. Modern "communities," however, are often inhabited by people who do not know one another at all. In a very real sense, therefore, many contemporary cities and towns are populated by strangers.

My student could not be known by her potential employer. There was little on which they could rely in deciding whether to trust her. She lived alone in a city far from Washington. The only assurances she could offer were minimal educational credentials and the recommendations of her professors and past employers. A drug test, a lie detector test, or any other form of preemployment test promised the bank a chance to reduce minimally the risks associated with hiring her.

The Costs of Privacy begins with this question: How, in an anonymous society of strangers, is trust possible? How are people able to trust others they have never met and do not know? The answer is that surveillance establishes reputations that permit us to trust strangers. Americans now enjoy vastly more privacy than in the past. But privacy makes it difficult to know much about other people; more privacy means more strangers. We are willing to trust those whose reputations justify that trust. So the question is: How are reputations established among strangers? Surveillance establishes and maintains reputations among strangers. Surveillance is defined as overt and conspicuous forms of credentials (e.g., credit cards, educational degrees, drivers' licenses) and/or ordeals (e.g., lie detector tests, drug tests, integrity tests). The use of such credentials and ordeals, over time, is shown to be correlated with the number of strangers in our society. Strangers are one of the costs of greater personal privacy. Surveillance is another cost.

The conclusion focuses on new methods of surveillance that can record genetic and biochemical information about people. Unlike traditional bases of reputation, genetic information makes it possible to predict physical illnesses, mental health problems, and various types of behavior. The same drug test my former student took to monitor past behavior also could have been used to predict future "problems" for her employer. These new forms of surveillance may seem attractive because they make it possible to enter into risky relationships with many more people (i.e., trust them) without ever getting to know them. This has the potential to alter public life in subtle, although important, ways. And that may be the greatest cost of privacy.

I have been the lucky beneficiary of much assistance with this project. My colleagues Paul Kingston, Ted Caplow, Gresham Sykes, and Donald Black read the manuscript at various stages of its preparation and offered advice and criticism. My colleague Gianfranco Poggi provided references and copies of related works by scholars in his international network. Professor Joe Harder of the Wharton School of Management offered many relevant sources after reading the chapter on preemployment screening and testing. Professor Sandra Schmidt of the University of Virginia McIntire School of Commerce offered valuable assistance and materials on employment testing. Professor Joseph Kett endured several lengthy luncheon conversations about the project and provided valuable references on the historical meaning of privacy. Graduate students in my seminar on the family read and critiqued the manuscript in depth. My very talented graduate student, Marian Borg, helped me develop my ideas as she pursued her dissertation on a related topic.

I was especially fortunate to benefit from the detailed comments and criticisms of my colleague, Jeffrey Hadden. For his time and attention to the various drafts of this manuscript, his care and concern with logic and argument and his sense of humor, I am deeply grateful.

Many individuals provided needed materials along the way. Walter Newsome, head of Government Documents at the University of Virginia, was of invaluable assistance in locating historical census materials on living arrangements and educational attainment. Jack Goodman and Glenn Canner of the Federal Reserve System provided materials on consumer credit and credit card use. Suzanne Bianchi of the U.S. Bureau of the Census helped locate missing Current Population Surveys from the late 1940s and early 1950s. Andrew Moncrief of Mediamark Research, Inc. provided results of national surveys of credit card users. Catherine Cortelyou, Public Service Librarian at the University of California, Berkeley, discovered several items on drivers licensing. To all these generous colleagues I offer my sincere thanks.

To those at Aldine de Gruyter, I offer my heartiest thanks. Jim Wright, series editor and friend, gave the initial impetus to move this book into his series. Richard Koffler, Executive Editor, was very helpful in his work with me during the review and revision stages of the work. And Arlene Perazzini was a constant source of help in the production of the book. To these delightful colleagues I give my deepest thanks.

My deepest gratitude is reserved for my wife, Daphne Spain. She read every version of the manuscript. She offered the critical eye of a sociologist and editor. And on countless occasions she listened and offered the help that was needed. I count myself among the luckiest of people to have both a friend and professional colleague as my partner.

1

INTRODUCTION

How, in an anonymous society of strangers, is trust produced? How do people transact business, extend or receive credit, select their doctors, or hire employees when the parties to such exchanges do not know one another? How can people board airplanes, buses, and taxicabs driven by total strangers confident that their safety is not in jeopardy?

More generally, how is it possible to depend on or believe in other people when we have never met them? We trust those who, we believe, accept and abide by the same moral rules we do; people who are known to *conform* to those standards we hold as important. Those who refuse to play by those rules or those we are not sure about are not so likely to be trusted. We suspect them. We doubt their word.

In this book I will argue that historically, increasing numbers of strangers produced greater and more pervasive personal privacy. Modern Americans enjoy vastly more privacy than did their forebears because ever and ever larger numbers of strangers in our lives are legitimately denied access to our personal affairs. Changes in familial living arrangements are largely responsible for these trends. Privacy, however, makes it difficult to form reliable opinions of one another. Legitimately shielded from other's regular scrutiny, we are thereby more immune to the routine monitoring that once formed the basis of our individual reputations. Reputation, I will argue, is a necessary and basic component of the trust that lies at the heart of social order. To establish and maintain reputations in the face of privacy, social mechanisms of *surveillance* have been elaborated or developed. In particular, various forms of credentials and modern ordeals produce reputations that are widely accessible, impersonal, and portable from one location to another. *A society of strangers is one of immense personal privacy. Surveillance is the cost of that privacy.*

Trust and the ability to take others at their word are basic ingredients in social order. If we never knew who to trust, could never be sure that what we were told was true, or that promises made would be promises kept, there would be little to bind us together or make groups cohesive. A collection of soloists who pursued their individualistic ends without respect to conventional standards and moral obligations would amount

1

to little more than a random grouping of people. Such a group would not constitute an organization or society. Trust, in short, lies at the base of any cohesive collectivity. Therefore, the extent to which trust among people is possible determines, in part, the degree of solidarity to be found in any society.

In their ordinary day-to-day lives, people frequently organize their behaviors by reference to their own and others' reputations. A reputation is a shared, or collective, perception about a person. It is the product of innumerable contacts among and between people. Through our dealings with others, an image is developed of the degree to which we do or do not conform to the standards that matter to them. Those who enjoy a "good" reputation are thought to accept and abide by those standards—perhaps even demonstrating extraordinary conformity to them. The highly respected civic leader is one who has shown a willingness or desire to accept selflessly the burdens of duty to others. In so doing, such a person has conformed to a value shared by members of the community. That person will be trusted. His word is believed; his promise accepted.

If we try to imagine a society without reputations, of anonymous strangers, it is a frightening image. Among those we know, much of our behavior is governed by reputation. We know to distrust the well-known scoundrel as surely as we believe a priest. *Reputation is a mantle worn with clear consequences for others' behaviors.* Deserved or not, a bad reputation marks someone as an outsider—beyond the ordinary boundaries of our own moral community. Strangers, however, present us with a dilemma not encountered when dealing with a person who enjoys a good or bad reputation.

When someone has no reputation, that person is a stranger. We don't trust strangers as much as people whose reputations are known. Strangers are suspect and must demonstrate that they can be trusted— that they respect and abide by the same rules we do—before they will be embraced as members of any group. Strangers must *earn* other peoples' trust. To do that, they must somehow earn a good reputation.

No matter how difficult it may be to earn a good reputation, the problem for a person with a *bad* reputation is usually much worse. A bad reputation marks someone as an outsider—as someone who might not respect the important standards of a group or community. Just as a good reputation opens doors, a bad reputation closes them. And just as one must earn a good reputation, so too, a bad reputation must be earned.

Conformity to group standards is necessary to earn a good reputation. A bad reputation is usually the product of having been shamed. And there are powerful incentives to avoid shame because once shamed, there are few ways to absolve the bad reputation. One must either renounce the group doing the shaming, or redefine the self in accordance with the group standards, that is, one must either leave or change one's ways. Given what is required to undo a bad reputation, and given the consequences of having one, we may assume that there is powerful incentive to avoid earning one. Shame, or the threat of it, in other words, is a form of social control; a collective method of enforcing conformity or punishing deviance.

So long as people know one another, good and bad reputations guide much of their social life. But what about complex societies where very few people are known; where the overwhelming majority of other people are strangers? How, in such a society, can we know whether to trust the strangers we deal with on a regular day-to-day basis? *How can we trust the people we see but do not know; those who live near us, who work near us, who must sometimes be counted on to help us?* That is the question I address in this book.

The answer to this question is that complex societies have produced impersonal arrangements that establish or maintain individual reputations—both good and bad. These reputations, unlike that of the civic leader in the small community, are easily transportable. They do not depend on a particular locale or group. They follow us as we move and they are accessible when they are needed. They can be altered, or created, in a matter of minutes. Reputations, in short, have become portable in our times just like other forms of capital ("human," or otherwise).

There are two methods used to establish or maintain reputations among modern strangers; *credentials* and *ordeals*. Together these constitute the two elementary forms of overt *surveillance*. Surveillance of this sort (overt) is directed, primarily or solely, at reputations. And although credentials and ordeals may be useful for other purposes, their role in establishing reputations is the most important use.

Before going into detail about surveillance, it will help to consider the proposed reason for it—*strangers*. My argument states that it is the presence of strangers that calls forth surveillance. I will argue that recent decades have been periods of significant and rapid growth in both the numbers of strangers and in both types of overt surveillance.

What does it mean to say there has been a growth in the number of strangers? We may assume that so long as there have been large societies there have been many people who were not known to one another. I argue, however, that there are more strangers now than in the past, primarily as a result of changes in our living arrangements.

Historically individuals have been given opportunities to openly demonstrate their willingness to abide by the rules; in open congregational "relations" (confessions required for admission to the church), through ordinary and regular contacts with public officials (constables or "tithing-men" who were charged with monitoring the coming and going of members of a community's households), and many other public forums. But more than any other traditional source of reputation, the family has been the most important. As sociologists would say, the family is the source of a person's *ascriptive status;* one's initial location in society. The child born two centuries ago to a laborer began life with a name and social position. That position reflected the general appraisal of the father in the community—his reputation and social standing. Traditional family government relied on patriarchs to enforce community standards. Prior to the establishment of an official civic police force (middle nineteenth century) his was the dominant authority, and, if shared, was shared with a representative of a church. For most of our history a person was known, first, by his or her family name. The family "name" served as a reputation among those familiar with one another.

The most notorious criminals frequently are described by the media as "loners," unknown by neighbors and unconnected to family. When deviance of virtually any sort is discovered, we look for its causes in the deviant's family situation because the family has served as the dominant form of social control in all societies. Embedded within their parents' or their own families, individuals are subject to many demands not made on people who live alone. By custom and law, the head of the household has been held accountable for the actions of all members of the family. Husbands have been required to settle the debts of their wives just as parents have been required to compensate others for the wrongful actions of their children. But family members have also been held accountable for the actions of the patriarch. In nineteenth century America, wives and children were held legally accountable for the unsettled debts of the head of the household.

The methods by which families control the behaviors of their members are diverse. To summarize these, sociologists refer to socialization—the process by which we learn the ways of a social group so that we can function within it. Socialization is a concept that summarizes the learning of numerous skills and motives that result in conformity (Elkin and Handel, 1984:4). The irreducible minimum requirement for socialization is another person; interaction is the core around which all theories of socialization are based. But what is it about interaction that produces conformity?

Supervision, or surveillance, is one unremarkable element that explains a vast amount of conformity in any society. Supervision establishes reputations. I hope to show that as traditional methods of family supervision decline, institutional methods of surveillance arise that serve the same social control functions. It is the relationship between trends in familial living arrangements and trends in surveillance that occupies the core of this book.

For the past 50 years in America, growing numbers of individuals have, for one reason or another, formed independent, nonfamily living arrangements. Several demographic trends have contributed to this outcome. Among the elderly, differential male/female life expectancy (females outlive males) combined with age heterogamy in marriage (husbands are typically 2 to 3 years older than their wives) result in significant numbers of widows who maintain their own homes after their husbands die. Thirty-six percent of all women 65 to 74 are widowed; 9 percent of men are (U.S. Bureau of the Census,1991a, Table 1). Among middle-aged (35 to 45 years old) individuals, high rates of marital disruption produce separate households (usually temporary) for the formerly married (32 percent of women this age are known to have been divorced) (U.S.Bureau of the Census, 1990, Table A).

Another trend of even greater significance has produced solitary living arrangements among Americans. There is now a new and historically unique stage of the life course that intervenes between that of adolescence (when children live at home with their parents) and adulthood (when grown children establish their own families). Beginning in the 1960s, large numbers of youths began to leave their parents' home to establish independent households. Although an historic anomaly, so commonplace has the practice become that it is now considered routine or unexceptional. One in four males and one in five females 20 to 29 do not live in any form of family arrangement (U.S. Bureau of the Census, 1991a, Table 2). Though seemingly unremarkable as a stage in the life course of youth, it is quite remarkable in its consequences for our society.

For a period of several years, large numbers of young Americans live independently of their parents' families while not yet having established their own families. Lacking clearly defined and accepted standards of conduct, people who occupy this stage enjoy immense freedoms and privacies. No longer viewed as adolescents, and legally beyond the age of majority—legally "adults"—young people who live outside of any family setting constitute an entirely new social category in our society. Like any group of solitary individuals, this group of young people, whom I call the "emancipated," pose significant problems for social order.

Emancipation is a release from restraint or influence. When young men or women leave the parental home and strike out alone, they are freed from certain immediate influences over their behaviors. They are no longer subject to the direct parental supervision that was undoubtedly a part of their lives. Their comings and goings are less likely to be noticed. The rhythms of their daily routines are now hidden from parents' scrutiny. It is hard to know to what extent such emancipation might alter behaviors. But it is certainly reasonable to presume that greater freedom is one reason for seeking emancipation; young adults on their own are relatively immune from routine monitoring and that is a reason they are on their own.

Be it parent or spouse, the presence of intimate others in the home is a source of restraint on behaviors. The source of that restraint may be the sense of moral commitment that grows in conjugal relationships, the normative obligation to obey the wishes of parents, or the sense of responsibility that arises in dependent relationships. But it may also be little more than the scrutiny and supervision of others—a consequence of knowing that one's actions will be seen and evaluated.

There is nothing new about these observations. Family living has historically been required (by law or custom) of those who wished to participate fully in the social life of their communities. So when large numbers of people live otherwise, we are left to ponder whether something has been lost. Are the emancipated excluded from some measure of participation in social life? Is collective life less "orderly" by virtue of the presence of the emancipated? Is deviance more likely in a society where many people do not live with relatives? Is emancipation a problem for traditional methods of social control? I do not hope to address all such questions, though I believe each warrants scholarly research. There are many types of non family living: divorced, widowed, never-married. My primary concern is with the implications of independent living among the never married—of emancipation—for methods of sustaining social order and trust.

Emancipation has very obvious implications for the cohesiveness that binds us together as a society. The freedoms and privacies that accompany emancipation are direct evidence of ambiguous or unknown reputations. The privacy gained by living alone is the consequence of immunity from supervision. People who are not subject to direct scrutiny are also free from direct influence. *Those we do not watch, we do not know.* To restate this obvious point, the emancipated are less likely to have reputations. If reputations are the basis for trust, and trust a basis for social order, then the emancipated pose a problem. If we cannot know whether our neighbor or co-worker abides by the same rules we do, how can we trust them? If no one is watching over them, why should they rein in their deviant impulses? What makes them conform? Indeed, are people free from direct supervision as likely to obey the rules? That is the unanswered question that makes trusting them so problematic.

Sociology takes as axiomatic that in all but the very simplest of organizations or societies the external regulation of behavior (supervision and sanctions) must be supplemented by internal regulations—the learning of moral codes (or norms). No modern society can rely totally on external methods to enforce its rules. Individuals must be counted on to impose self-restraint, to *voluntarily* conform. Anthropologists and moral philoso-

phers distinguish between varying degrees of internal and external control when they contrast "shame" and "guilt" cultures—between those in
which external regulation is more or less effective in producing social
order. What distinguishes a "shame" from a "guilt" culture is that in the
former, public esteem is the greatest good, and to be ill spoken of the
greatest punishment. Public esteem, or the lack of it for the individual,
depends on that person's success or failure judged on the basis of some
code that embodies a group's values. Whoever fails to meet the demands
of that code ruins his reputation and loses the esteem of the other
members. He loses his honor; he earns a bad reputation.

In *small face-to-face groups*, shame is a fundamentally *social* thing.
Whereas guilt is quite personal, private, and internal, "shame is con-
nected with the thought that eyes are upon one" (Taylor, 1985:53). In a
shame culture, whoever fails to meet the demands of the code of honor
loses his good reputation. And where public honor (a good name or good
reputation) is of great importance, "if a man has lost his reputation, then
he has lost his value in the eyes of all the members of the group, and this
includes himself. . . . Being a member of the group entails being held in
esteem by the group, and being held in esteem entails both that certain
demands are made on him and that he has certain claims." To be shamed,
therefore, means the person is now viewed as having rejected those
claims and demands. This person can no longer be a member of the group
(Taylor, 1985:55–56).

In *large societies* shame is less central because people enjoy great
amounts of privacy. The "eye of the other" is less often a factor in how we
behave because often there is no other present. The greater emphasis on
"guilt" implies that modern societies inculcate strong incentives to conform even without the threat of immediate reactions from others for
failure to do so. Population density, mobility, and anonymity explain why
shame must be augmented by guilt. Shame "works" in face-to-face
groups. It works among those who know one another.

Guilt and shame are both quite powerful inducements to obey. But
unlike shame, guilt focuses on a particular deed or omission. The guilty
person has done something wrong. But it is his action (or inaction) on
which the guilt is focused. Simply because a person has broken *one* law, it
is not assumed that he has broken others. It is the particular *action*, not the
entire person that evokes the guilty reaction. The focus in shame is the kind
of person an individual is—not a specific action or omission. The guilty
person expects punishment for the wrong he has done. Indeed, punishment may resolve the guilt—that is, make up for what was done. But no
punishment will resolve shame because nothing can make up for the type
of person one is now shown to be. In shame, not an action, but the self of
the offender is the focus of attention. Philosopher Gabriele Taylor con-

trasts guilt and shame by comparing them to "primary" and "secondary" deviance—Edwin Lemert's distinction between actions an individual views as wrong though not central to his sense of who he is, and actions that reflect the fundamental type of person one is. "When feeling shame, I see myself as being all of a piece, what I have just done fits only too well with what I really am. When feeling guilty, I think of myself as having brought about a forbidden state of affairs and in this respect disfigured a self which otherwise remains the same" (Taylor, 1985:92).

The distinction between secrecy and privacy helps to explain the importance of surveillance as it pertains to shame and guilt. Privacy implies a legitimate denial of access while secrecy implies that the denial of access is illegitimate. We are entitled to our privacy, but not to secrecy (Warren and Laslett, 1977). For the past 20 years, privacy has been safeguarded as a Constitutional right of Americans—a privilege that may be abridged only in the face of "compelling" interests of the state. There are, in short, actions and areas deemed legitimately beyond scrutiny by the state or by uninvited others. This is the interpretation of the Bill of Rights made by the U.S. Supreme Court in Griswald v. Connecticut (1965). That we acknowledge such areas and protect them by Constitutional guarantees is clear evidence of our trust in one another. Yet it is also evidence of *how far* we are willing to trust one another. For just as we acknowledge private spheres, we recognize the existence of secrecy. Sexual behaviors between heterosexual couples, contraceptive usage, and abortion are examples of domains of behavior *now* (though not historically) defined as private in our society. Secrecy, in contrast, refers to hidden actions that are "illegitimate." Shame and guilt pertain to *secret* things, not to *private* things.

The distinction between the secret and the private is always a matter for negotiation. Things once secret (e.g., abortion) are now private and things once private (wife beating) are now secret. In the aggregate, a society might be characterized by the amount of things that are defined as secret or private. The resulting amount of each type of action would locate the society at some point along the shame/guilt culture continuum. In a pure (and therefore hypothetical) shame culture, there is little privacy. Very little would be *legitimately* beyond public scrutiny because shame presumes complete knowledge about another's actions. In modern societies, however, there is widespread privacy. In *The Economics of Justice*, Posner (1981) speculated that the transition from "shame" to "guilt" culture is correlated with the ease of maintaining privacy. Ridicule, public songs recounting a villain's misdeeds, or other public rituals (i.e., charivari) are well-known methods by which people in small (shame) societies make grievances public, seek public support, and shame an opponent in public (Krygier, 1983).

To shame another, that person must be known and must be a member of the group applying the shame. An outsider, or stranger, cannot be shamed this way. *The relative absence of privacy in a society is correlated with the relative absence of strangers.* As Flaherty (1972) noted about colonial America, prior to 1750 virtually everyone lived in towns under 1,500 (even if they farmed). Prohibitions against solitary living meant that unmarried people lived as boarders or lodgers in other's households. Everyone was known by virtually everyone else since with only 1,500 people there are not that many families. In such a situation, anonymity was virtually impossible. Things done in front of others were known to reflect on peoples' reputations and those of their families. Things are very different when anonymity is possible. As Martin Krygier has noted, there are occasions in complex industrial societies when anonymity is *not* possible. But even where it is not, "one can often separate the contexts in which one plays different social roles without fear, for example, of one's public 'self' being undermined by the face one exposes in private. The situation is radically different in small, face-to-face societies. Unless particular precautions are taken, *all behavior is public behavior*" (Krygier, 1983:315, emphasis added). In a close-knit society of intimates, friends, neighbors, and associates social life involves frequent, perhaps almost constant submission to the judgment of peers. It is difficult then to "live down" one's reputation because it is difficult to change villages, jobs, or associates.

People are more likely to seek escape from the watchful eye of strangers than of intimates. Escape from the watchful eye of intimates is more often solitude, isolation, or loneliness perhaps, but not as often privacy. This is not to deny that there is privacy among intimates. Even in the most cramped of quarters, family members are able to acknowledge others' rightful escape from constant scrutiny. Most often, however, what we do not reveal to intimates are secrets. Escape from the scrutiny of strangers is, however, privacy. This point is made clearly by anthropologist Jean Briggs' account of life in an Utku igloo.

The Utku, a simple society of Eskimo Indians, live in extremely close quarters—for months restricted to life inside an igloo. In such an existence, extremely little (not sex or bodily evacuation) escapes observation by others. In such a society, to be *removed* from such contact—from the ever-present watchful eyes of intimates—is a punishment, a privation as great as any social sanction available (Briggs, 1970) Among the Utku, "there is no distinction between public and private spheres and concerns" (Briggs, 1970:13). And as Barrington Moore has observed: "Without the public, nothing can be private" (Moore, 1984:21). *For privacy to have any real meaning, there must be strangers.* Intimacy may be thought of as the opposite of privacy. Without strangers, one's confidential actions are more likely to be secret—not private. Viewed this way, the movement from shame to guilt culture occurs with the growth and presence of strangers. Stated differently, the distinction between privacy and secrecy depends on the role of strangers. When applied to an entire society, the aggregate amount of behaviors that are private or secret is clearly related to the composition of the population: *When there are more strangers, there is more privacy.*

But the very presence of strangers means that there are those without easily known reputations. Strangers, in other words, must be subject to social mechanisms of overt surveillance—mechanisms designed to produce reputations. Thus, *when there are more strangers, it is more likely that there will be overt surveillance.*

In his cross-cultural analysis of privacy, Moore described privacy as an escape from obligations. He argued that such an escape is possible only to the extent that individuals do not depend *directly* on broad societal cooperation. Individuals may not demand the right to escape or to withdraw from society when all individuals depend directly on each other's participation. In advanced societies, privacy is more possible because there are far more powerful means of enforcing unity and repressing dissent—of ensuring that things get done (Moore, 1984:74). Privacy exists when others' actions have little consequence for us—they may be good or bad, but regardless, they have little import for us. Clearly, therefore, the existence of privacy presupposes either a more or less loosely knit *moral community*—one in which individual actions may not be directly relevant to all—or an economic arrangement in which continuous mutual cooperation is unnecessary.

Ancient Hebrew culture lacked pervasive privacy because any members' transgressions, it was believed, brought consequences from Yaweh. Theirs was a very tightly bound moral community. The Eskimos studied by Briggs lacked privacy because their economy demanded continuous cooperation and collaboration to secure the things needed for the community (fish and game). Modern society is typically both loosely bound (morally) and structured around an economy that does not require continuous mutual cooperation. Extensive privacy, therefore, is possible.

Colonial New England is another instructive case to consider. Indeed, the historical record of American privacy is clear in showing how the *increase* in privacy (and strangers) was accompanied by an increase in overt forms of surveillance. As privacy increased, overt surveillance developed apace.

In his analysis of privacy in Colonial New England, David Flaherty (1972) argues that privacy was institutionalized and recognized. But we would hardly recognize it as such by today's standards. The extent to which everyday behavior was monitored was impressive. Most notably, there were virtually no *anonymous* individuals prior to the end of the eighteenth century. Laws governed whether one could move to an area, when one could be outdoors (not at night), what one could say in public, and what one could wear in public (sumptuary laws).

A vast array of informal arrangements established clearly an individual's reputation in the community. By this I mean that these arrangements were structured around everyday life, and carried on by members of the community. Church attendance was mandatory, enforced by law, until the Revolution. Each town elected 5 to 10 "wardens" to enforce Sabbath laws. Ministers' duties included, expressly, surveillance functions. For example, he visited taverns and rooted out the "tipplers." Full membership in a church (required to receive the sacrament of Holy Communion) required an examination for membership. This examination, known as "the relation," was conducted by the minister and by the congregation. The subject was required to confess past sins and recount how God had affected their lives. As Flaherty (1972:141) notes: "The procedures (to enter the Puritan church) seem to have authorized compulsory disclosure of intimate matters and searching forays into private lives." Given the tremendous pressure to become a full member of the Church (in a theocracy), the Relation was, for all intents and purposes, mandatory. But such public confessions, although the subject of increasing debate as the eighteenth century wore on, served to subject many people to public scrutiny, thereby reinforcing or establishing a public reputation. Moreover, the existence and acceptance of such a principle justified Church and community surveillance. New England Puritans saw their personal religious duty as requiring that they watch over *each other*.

These strategies became less and less effective with time and population growth. After the Revolution, for example, the "relation" was gradually abolished. In place of these informal structures, there arose overt methods of establishing reputations—methods that did not rely on a close-knit community.

Privacy grows as the number of strangers grows. And since strangers do not have reputations, there will be more surveillance when there are more strangers. *Privacy is one consequence, or cost, of growing numbers of strangers. Surveillance is one consequence, or cost, of privacy.*

The proposition that privacy is *more* widespread than it was in the past deserves greater elaboration. Modern data storage and retrieval systems arouse justifiable concerns over privacy and the possibility that it is threatened. The ability to computerize individual biographies (or portions of them) makes the storage and use of such information less costly and vastly more efficient than were parish records or more informal systems of record-keeping. However, the *ability* to store, access, and use biographical information is not the main factor in the expansion or restriction of privacy. Privacy results from the legitimate denial of *access* to one's actions or records. Privacy is defined by the socially-recognized legitimate right to restrict others from observing or knowing about one's actions.

To know whether Americans enjoy more or less privacy today than their ancestors did, one would have to determine whether there has been an increase or a decrease in the range of behaviors and circumstances legitimately defined as beyond the scrutiny of uninvited others. In the course of a typical day, are modern Americans better able to escape the watchful eyes of others than their grandparents were? Are there more opportunities to seclude oneself behind closed doors than there once were? Are more areas of life legitimately viewed as beyond others' scrutiny? I have already argued that the answer to these questions is yes. Others have come to similar conclusions (see, for example, Shils, 1966; Sennett, 1978; Parsons, 1971; Brill, 1990; Halpern, 1992).

Edward Shils (1966:282) provides a guide to answering this question when he notes that "privacy exists where the persons whose actions engender or become the objects of information retain possession of that information, and any flow outward of that information from the persons to whom it refers occurs on the initiative of its possessors." A "violation" of privacy, therefore, involves the "acquisition or transmission of information without the voluntary consent or initiative of those whose actions and words generate the information." This definition of privacy directs us to see it as a *relationship* rather than a property. Privacy refers to relationships in which people retain possession of something that might otherwise be shared, and if shared, is shared on the initiative or with the consent of the "possessor." Shils observes that very personal information *is*, on occasion, illegitimately revealed. But when such revelations are voluntary or when the information was not obtained by deceit or subterfuge, he suggests that we speak of a *sharing of privacy* rather than a violation of it.

Shils (1966:282) argues that urbanization and industrialization in the nineteenth century increased the amount of privacy enjoyed by average citizens. By "amount," he means "the proportion of their total range of activity and thought that was disclosed only to those to whom the actor chose to disclose it." The forces that produced more privacy are well-known. The stimulation of an urban environment drew attention away from intimate affairs and toward public events. The mobility of the population, the separation of home and work, rising standards of "respectability" that stressed the importance of reserve and respect for the individual, and Victorian attitudes toward sexuality fostered greater privacy. And the growing diversity of religious sects meant that people were less likely to share information about one another because they were members of different congregations. A growing acceptance of solitary living also meant that by the turn of the twentieth century, few households contained boarders or lodgers.

Notable technological changes have contributed to greater privacy. Modern conveniences such as the telephone, television, washer, dryer, air conditioner, and VCR make it less necessary for individuals to leave their homes to venture into public. Televisions, radios, and videotape machines produce entertainment that is enjoyed behind closed doors. Washers and dryers mean that people no longer hang their laundry out to dry and make fewer trips to commercial laundries. Air conditioning reduces the need to sit on the front porch, visit public lakes, swimming pools, or parks. Telephones reduce the need to visit others in person (Popenoe, 1985).

New methods of information-gathering and dissemination by employers, creditors, and governments that strike many as worrisome, are not necessarily violations of privacy. These developments have occurred in the name of objectives that are widely regarded as legitimate: freedom of the press, the protection of public order, the prevention of subversion, and administrative efficiency. Each has been generally accepted as reasonable and useful. Almost all depend on voluntary self-disclosure (the completion of credit, insurance or drivers license, or employment forms, for example). Disclosure of such information is not a violation of privacy unless it is given to parties to whom an individual does not want it made available.

There *are* limits, or boundaries, implied in the granting of personal information. Only when those limits, or boundaries, are exceeded is privacy violated. Such limits are, in fact, exceeded sometimes. However, it is *that* transgression that implies a violation of privacy, not simply the collection or dissemination of information, no matter how widespread or rapidly it is done. The existence of a centralized, computerized, record of all Americans, for example, would not represent an intrusion or violation of privacy. Only if the information contained in that system was made available against an individual's wishes, or if that information were obtained without consent could we speak of a violation of a person's privacy. Similarly, the sale of mailing lists to marketers may, or may not, be a violation of privacy depending on what limits of dissemination were understood by those who provided their names and addresses to begin with.

I will argue that the extensiveness of privacy and surveillance are strongly related phenomena. There are probably limits to how extensive each may become. But it is crucial to acknowledge that both the access to, and dissemination of information about people are *social processes* governed by cultural beliefs and normative standards of *trust*. It is certainly legitimate to be concerned about the elaboration of computerized methods of monitoring and tracking people. The use of those techniques, however, is governed by widespread standards of propriety and personal autonomy. It is also related to our concerns about trusting strangers and our need to enter into risky relationships with them. A sociological appreciation of the relationship between privacy and surveillance will provide a new way of thinking about the "threat" of an all-knowing state or employer.

Privacy grows as the number of strangers grows. Strangers are those whose reputations we cannot know, not solely those people who are isolated from one another. Two people who have never met, and who never will, certainly are strangers to each another. But it is our diminished *ability* to know about others that has led to an increase in the prevalence of strangers. The same forces that Shils credits for having increased our privacy may be seen as having increased our ability to restrict others' scrutiny of our affairs. By enforcing our autonomy (or privacy), we safeguard our reputations. We may, if we choose, elect to remain strangers to many others; that is what our privacy permits, and is one reason it is desired. That is also one reason for the increase in surveillance.

Overt surveillance consists of credentials and ordeals. Each is a means by which the basis for trust may be established, and are dealt with at length in later chapters. I wish to define these terms briefly now before continuing.

Credentials

A credential is something that gives a person access to credit or confidence. Credentials may certify many things: competence, completion of a course of study, membership in formal or voluntary associations, or credit-worthiness. Credentials announce to others that a person has established a claim to membership in a recognized group of similar individuals. And, by definition, a credential certifies an individual as a recognizable type of person—one who accepts and abides by certain principles. Seen this way, credentials are part of an individual's public reputation—sometimes the only visible portion of public reputation.

Certain public rituals confer the equivalent of credentials. An individual may publicly embrace convention by participating in a ritual that confers, more or less, a symbolic credential. A marriage ceremony, for example, establishes an individual as having both a legal and a social status different from single people. Historically, public baptisms, oral examinations, and routine public meetings have been used to confer membership, discover deviance, or administer sanctions—in short to establish the equivalent of a credential. Sociologist Michael Hechter

(1987:50–56) argues that consensual decision-making in meetings is a method whereby private beliefs and attitudes become known—a form of surveillance.

Successful performance in the economy may produce outward symbols that serve as credentials—conspicuous signs of success. The ability to demonstrate success outwardly is taken as a sign of membership—as a symbol of adequate participation. Indeed, for most of our associates, reputation is established by such things as occupational status or other visible signs of achievement. Philosopher Agnes Heller has argued that success is increasingly the basis of reputation—perhaps the dominant basis in modern society. Lack of success, she has argued, is the cause for shame. "The gods of shame culture were pleased by a successful warrior, but only if success had been attained in keeping with the code of honor. In our times, being successful is dissociated from the totality of behavior for the simple reason that the latter is no longer visible. Only success is visible, therefore (increasingly) it is in this respect alone that the Other's Eye will approve or disapprove of persons" (Heller, 1985:18).

Conspicuous examples of credentials include educational and/or professional degrees, credit cards that permit validation of one's credit-worthiness at the point of sale, or driver's licenses that serve as universally recognized proof of identification and also certify one as minimally competent to drive.

Ordeals

I define an ordeal as a ritual that determines whether an individual is telling the truth. It always begins with a presumption of guilt or unresolvable doubt. All ordeals submit the question at hand to a supernatural, or nonhuman power. Rarely, if ever, is the "truth" revealed by an ordeal appealed because there is no higher power. It is only when a person's word is in doubt that ordeals are employed. As such, their direct and immediate object is individual reputation. Through an ordeal people are able to validate their reputation, to garner proof of the validity of their claims, or to establish their claim to *innocence*, membership, or competence. Commonplace examples of ordeals include drug tests, lie-detector tests, and obligatory confessions in communes or churches. By "passing" an ordeal, one establishes or sustains a claim to membership in the group endorsing the ordeal.

Mizruchi (1983) argues that the existence of large numbers of relatively unattached and unintegrated people leads to the emergence of social structures to contain them—what he calls "abeyance" structures. Compulsory schooling, for example, emerged to accommodate large numbers of adolescents when such individuals were not well integrated into the world of work. There were not adequate "status vacancies" to absorb the population for which the abeyance structure emerged. "The underlying concern was with unattached and unintegrated youth. The traditional apprenticeship system in the United States began to contract during the early nineteenth century, just as the cities began to expand. In addition to the rural migrants, immigrants from Europe now contributed to the vast numbers of new urban dwellers. Compulsory attendance at school was one sure way to organize and indoctrinate these potentially wayward youth" (Mizruchi, 1983:119). Compulsory schooling, therefore, provided surveillance.

Any method of social control depends, immediately, on information about individuals. More specifically, in every historical period, information about conformity to conventional standards of conduct and thought is the starting point for any response to deviance. There can be no social control without such information.

But neither can there be trust. In the following chapters I explore the history of emancipation, and the role of credentials and ordeals in the establishment and maintenance of reputations among the emancipated.

2

EMANCIPATION OF YOUTH

Introduction

When young men or women are emancipated from their parents' homes, they are subjected to much less scrutiny. Their parents have much less direct influence over their daily behaviors. Much, if not all, of their ordinary life is now free from parental supervision. Things once noticed now go unseen. Things previously prohibited are now possible. Indeed, the freedom from watchful eyes is one of the reasons young people leave home to strike out on their own. It is, therefore, quite reasonable to suppose that emancipated youths will behave differently once they have left home. Free from routine scrutiny by parents, the person no longer living in their parents' home may enjoy much greater privacy and freedom. But they might not.

The real question is what sort of living arrangement follows leaving the parental nest. Virtually all children leave home eventually; some for jobs and some for college. But regardless of the reason, many leave only to form another household with a spouse or cohabiting partner. This has been the traditional pattern of leaving the parental home; to form another household with a spouse. As anthropologists might say, the family of "orientation" (the family into which one is born) is typically replaced by a family of "procreation" (the family created through marriage). Doubtless there are substantial differences between living with one's parents and one's spouse. But in neither case is an individual's domestic life free from routine and regular monitoring or supervision. Be it parent or spouse, the presence of intimate others in the home is a source of restraint on behaviors. The source of that restraint may be the sense of moral commitment that grows in conjugal relationships, the normative obligation to obey the wishes of parents, or the sense of responsibility that arises in intimate relationships. But it may also be little more than the scrutiny and supervision of others—a consequence of knowing that one's actions will be seen. Historically, almost all adults have spent most of their entire lives in such family-like arrangements.

17

By contrast, growing numbers of young people today leave home to strike out *alone;* living in households with neither conjugal nor blood relatives—often with no other person at all. These young people, the "emancipated," represent an entirely new and unique phase of the life course. Prior to this century in America, there were virtually no young people who lived apart from kin. Immediate or distant relatives have traditionally been co-residents with young people until they married—an arrangement strongly conditioned by cultural norms or law—for good reason.

Single young people are perceived to pose a threat to stable systems of social relations. Their freedom and autonomy have traditionally been limited because they might threaten existing marriages with the possibility of adultery. Sexual misalliances involving unmarried people have been the subject of some of the most intense and public forms of social and legal sanctions. More generally, in the absence of parental or spousal supervision, young people have often been seen as a potential threat to many legal and moral conventions. Crimes, for example, are more often committed by the young, and crime rates fluctuate with the proportion of the population in their teen years (Nock and Kingston, 1990:246–248). Whether unsupervised youths *are,* in fact, such a threat is much less important than the perception that they are. Young people are treated differently because "mature" adults suspect that if limits are not imposed, youths will do things they should not do. Their privacy (legitimate immunity from the scrutiny of others)—unchecked by responsible co-residents—permits widespread secrecy (illegitimate escape from surveillance). And secrecy in all cultures must be prevented, or uncovered.

Not bound by the constraints of family responsibility young bachelors (especially) and spinsters have historically been forbidden to live free from the routine supervision of kin or other adults. Colonial settlements forbade or fined heavily the practice of solitary living. Indeed, early American settlements had no housing reserved for single people. Boarding with another family was the preferred solution to having no immediate kin to live with. The Colonists appreciated the potentially liberating influence of living apart from kin. And they made sure that the practice was not likely to happen.

At the turn of the Twentieth Century in America, fewer than 3 percent of males under age 24 were not living in families (with parents or spouse). By 1990 that percentage had climbed to almost 25 percent. In this chapter I discuss the various forces that contributed to the growth of the "emancipated" population this century. This history shows that there was no single factor responsible for the creation of this new stage in the life course. Instead, many often related forces reshaped the form that nest leaving took. Perhaps most centrally, economic changes associated with industrialization made emancipation a possibility. But lengthened educational requirements, changing ideas about human development, and various demographic changes have also contributed to this change in the life course of individuals.

The history of the "emancipated" is also the history of growing amounts of autonomy among young people. The greater freedom granted to young people today in their living arrangements is also reflected in marriage and employment. Increasingly, matrimony and work are areas over which young people have gained greater and greater individual freedom of choice. Indeed, mate selection in the United States is known throughout the world as governed foremost by individual choice. So too, decisions about where and when one will work are typically individual choices made on the basis of personal decisions.

Autonomy, privacy, freedom, and choice are all words that signal an absence of control. To the extent that young people are "free" to live on their own, they are also free from much of the control once exercised within the walls of the family home. No matter how minimal parents' rules of conduct within the parental home, the simple presence of adults with nominal responsibility can be assumed to have curbed children's wild impulses. Simply knowing that one is being watched alters behaviors. So long as young people live at home, they are governed by their ascriptive reputations. They may enjoy privileges or suffer privations because of their family name. If a 16 year old gets into trouble, her parents are held morally and legally accountable. What about a 19 year old? Even when beyond the age of majority, young people's actions may be blamed on their parents if they live at home.

When a 20 year old leaves home and rents his first apartment across town from his parents, he becomes more responsible for his actions. Correspondingly, his parents become less responsible. This is so because we know that when a person does not live under the same roof, it is very hard to monitor his actions and even harder to keep him in line. Living apart from parents might be expected to foster different behaviors and beliefs. The intergenerational link is weakened and, as a result, the controlling ability of parents is reduced. Who keeps this young man in line once he moves out from his parents' home? How is supervision possible? Is it possible?

These are new questions; ones that were not asked in earlier historical eras. Controlling young people has always been something of a problem, of course. But when they lived in a family—their parents' or their own—the problems were qualitatively different. The simple presence of large numbers of unattached adults means that social control becomes more difficult. Without the routine surveillance of others, how is conformity enforced? What is the source of normative pressure to abide by the rules?

And how can we know whether to trust someone we have never met or heard about—someone living alone and not part of any family? How can we deal with someone like this who has no known reputation? In light of the growth of the emancipated, is there a new order of social relations— have new means of control and supervision been established? In fact, overt surveillance is one response.

The Legal Concept of Emancipation

"Emancipation" is a basic concept of family law in America. Judicial emancipation refers to the termination of certain rights and obligations in the legal parent–child relationship during a child's minority (today defined as birth to age 18 or 19) (see Katz, Schroeder, and Sidman, 1973). In general terms, an emancipated child is one who has, with consent of his parent and/or the state, become his own decision maker for some purposes; the child might have reached a specified age or established a life independent of his parents through marriage, military service, or economic self-sufficiency (U.S. Department of Health and Human Services, 1981:29). Historically, American parents have been held legally responsible for a child's financial support, health, education, and the inculcation of basic attitudes (respect for people and authority). These obligations of parents are balanced by parents' legal *custody* of their children. Custody entitles the parent to discipline children, and to demand services (including wages and salaries). By order of a court, some or all of these rights and responsibilities may be no longer enforceable. In almost all instances of judicial emancipation, some amount of conflict between parents and the minor is involved. Rarely, that is, do both the parents and child agree that emancipation is desirable.

The legal basis for establishing an age of majority is that individuals younger than a certain age are not believed to be fully competent to run their own affairs. The law attempts to protect such individuals from harm or exploitation. The things that minors are not permitted to do are known as "disabilities" of minority. In almost every state they include the following prohibitions: establishing a separate domicile, retaining earnings, entering into binding contracts, consenting to medical or surgical care, suing or being sued in one's own name, suing parents for injuries, making a will, hiring an agent, entering into a partnership, or conveying real estate (U.S. Department of Health and Human Services, 1981.11).

A typical example of emancipation involves a minor who marries or enlists in the armed forces. In almost all states, a minor becomes emancipated when he or she enters into a valid marriage or joins the armed forces. Should the *parents* petition a court to be relieved of financial or other obligations, most courts will comply. In general, emancipation of minors is based on the parent's and not the minor's petition. Occasionally, however, the opposite is true. In the 1909 case of *Rounds Brothers v. McDaniel* a father asked that he receive his 18-year-old son's wages directly from the employer. The son had begun working at age 14 when he was living with his father and an aunt. At 16 he moved out and received no further support. From the time he moved out until the suit was brought the son had lived independently, spending his wages as he wished. The Supreme Court of Kentucky denied the father's request for his son's wages on the grounds that the son was emancipated by implication (i.e., the father's willingness to allow his son to move out of the home was, by implication, emancipation) [133 Ky. 669, 118 S.W. 956 (1909) (Katz et al., 1973:330]. In another case, a daughter who wanted to resume her education was able to return to the status of unemancipated minor for purposes of receiving support from her parent, even though the parent objected [*Turner v. Turner*, 441 S.W. 2nd 105 (Ky. 1969)].

A declaration of emancipation not only relieves a child of ordinary filial obligations (and privileges), but also of intrafamily tort immunities. Rarely are members of the same family permitted to bring tort suits (a tort is an action for which a civil suit may be brought) against one another. Family members are, generally, *immune* to tort suits by other members, though a minority of states (18) have abrogated that rule. However, the emancipated minor or his or her parents may initiate a civil suit against the other. It is this issue that is most frequently the cause of legal emancipation—will the intrafamily tort immunity rule bar a law suit?

The doctrine of emancipation was rarely used prior to the turn of the twentieth century. It was only when our economy permitted easy migration and full economic independence that a child's legal separation from its parents emerged as a significant legal issue. When children worked in family enterprises (farming or small businesses) they were viewed legally as their parents' property.

> Since child labor was crucial to the economic system, the parental right to a minor child's services and wages was also a practical necessity. In such a hierarchical and tightly structured system, breaking the tie of duty and obligation between parents and child was unthinkable. . . . [At the turn of this century] the belief in the ability of the individual to strike out on his own and through hard work and persistence become a 'success' reached its zenith. In this atmosphere, the family lost some of its cohesiveness. The legal sanctioning of some limited mobility out of the family was compatible with and even responsive to the economic needs and cultural tenor of the times. (Katz et al., 1973:328).

As legal scholar Sanford Katz has argued, judicial emancipation was handled on a case-by-case basis from 1900 to the early 1960s. The growing acceptance of state intervention and control of youths (the legal principle of *parens patriae*) this century, he argues, was accompanied by, if not a cause of, a growing willingness on the part of our courts to grant emancipation decrees. Still, so long as emancipation was handled on an individual basis, the practice was not widespread.

In the past 25 years, however, emancipation has assumed a different face. Rather than case-by-case decisions, emancipation has more recently been accomplished by *statute*. Such "statutory" emancipation refers to the removal of certain legal disabilities that are due to a person's age. Unlike judicial emancipation, the statutory variety refers to a partial elimination of the disabilities of age for an entire underage population rather than to specific individuals. Such broad changes in the legal meaning of age have been most conspicuous for only the past 25 years.

Most obvious was the passage of the twenty-sixth Amendment permitting 18 to 21 year olds to vote (passed in 1973). By 1980 every state except Mississippi had lowered its age of majority to 18 or 19. Once an individual attains the age of majority, all disabilities of minority are removed.

The right to seek medical treatment without parental consent has also been extended to minors. Beginning in the late 1960s, state legislatures passed statues permitting minors to seek and receive treatment for venereal disease, drug abuse problems, birth control, and abortion. Further, minors are now permitted to enter into binding legal contracts for educational loans and may be sued for defaulting on them. Some states permit minors to acquire automobile insurance in their own names or enter into binding contracts (professional sports contracts, for example).

In sum, since the mid-1960s, the age at which an individual becomes an adult has been significantly redefined. Prior to the passage of the twenty-sixth Amendment, an individual was not an adult—legally—before age 21 unless a court declared otherwise. The past two or three decades, however, have seen dramatic changes in the age at which an individual becomes an adult. As noted by a team of scholars who evaluated the legal status of adolescents in 1980

> Over the last ten [since 1970] years there has been, either consciously or unconsciously, an erosion of parental control. For example, the changing of the age of majority from 21 to 18 has removed the child from the control of the parents and allows the child full emancipation for all purposes upon reaching that age. Legislative and case law development of limited or partial emancipation likewise has continued this erosion of parental care, custody and control. (U.S. Department of Health and Human Services, 1981:25)

That youths grow up faster today than they did a century ago is hardly news. As a result of an industrial and service economy, independence is possible at earlier and earlier ages. And, of course, cultural beliefs have accompanied the changes in the economy. It is not so much that people leave home earlier. Indeed, the next section will show they do not. Rather, young people now establish independent lives that are free from families. For the first time in history, 20 year olds expect and are expected to live independently, neither living with their own parents nor maintaining their own families.

I will refer to youths who live in this fashion as the "emancipated." I do not refer to any particular *legal* status by my use of this term. Instead, I simply refer to the freedom from family obligations that today is an ordinary part of young adulthood but that 30 years ago was possible only by court order (and 100 years ago was inconceivable).

The emancipated are one very conspicuous group of "strangers." I do not wish to suggest that they are either the largest or most significant such category. Widowed, divorced, homeless, unemployed, and even remarried individuals are also, to varying degrees, "strangers" as I use that term. I focus on the emancipated because they represent a very *new category* of strangers. It is convenient to focus on youths in this way because it permits me to investigate changes that might be associated with the growth in their numbers.

The History of Emancipation

Nest leaving today typically occurs only once (although some recently divorced adult children do return to live with parents for a time only to leave again once they have attained economic and/or emotional stability). At some point in the life course an individual leaves home to establish a separate residence. Historically and until the mid-twentieth century, most young people remained in the parental home until marriage. However, nest leaving was not an abrupt event. Instead, most young people left and returned home several times. It was commonplace for children under 14 to live for a few months with neighbors, relatives, or others. These sojourns were for purposes of learning a trade ("putting out"), being tutored, attending academies in winter months (when children's labor was not so essential for agricultural pursuits), or earning money to help the family. As historian Joseph Kett noted, "semidependency" describes youths 10 to 21 in the early nineteenth century. Their dependence on parents lasted until approximately the same age as it does now. But there were intervals during which they lived with others prior to actually leaving home for good (Kett, 1977). "And since marriage was relatively late, this meant that they remained for a decade or more after completing their schooling to contribute to the family economy" (Goldscheider and DaVanzo, 1989:597). When young people left home prior to this century, it was to form a new family, or to live in some form of institutional housing (dormitories or lodging with another family) not to live alone. By contrast, in 1979, 72 percent of males and 59 percent of females left their parents home to live alone or with nonrelatives (Goldscheider and DaVanzo, 1989:605).

In the mid- and late twentieth century a new pattern of nest leaving with important consequences for living arrangements has emerged—the establishment of an independent household prior to marriage. "Such a life cycle pattern has been extremely rare, historically and comparatively" (Goldscheider and Goldscheider, 1987:278). The consequence of independent living arrangements for young adults is that "living in a family setting is now increasingly limited to sharply defined life cycle stages, married adults and minor children" (Goldscheider and Goldscheider, 1987:278). Undoubtedly, many factors have contributed to this dramatic change—especially the possibility of economic independence at youthful ages and rising expectations about higher education (sometimes leading to semiindependence in dormitories). Surprisingly, however, empirical analysis has shown that college attendance is not a factor of great importance. Demographers Goldscheider and LeBourdais concluded that the significant changes in nest leaving this century occurred primarily among *older* youths—those in their early twenties. "The proportions of children in their early twenties still living in their parents' home have been reduced between one third and one half" compared to only a 6 percent reduction for those age 18. "Those attending college were no more likely to leave early than those who did not" (Goldscheider and LeBourdais, 1986:143).

An analysis of a nationally representative sample of 28,000 high school students in 1980 revealed that over two-thirds of them (regardless of sex, race, religion, or socioeconomic status) *expect* to live independently before marriage. So, although recent in origin, the new pattern of nest leaving is "evidently a new normative requirement, one that young people may try hard to realize, and perhaps at considerable cost. To do so may require trading off on other expenses, such as those for marriage and for education" (Goldscheider and Goldscheider, 1987:284). In short, independent premarital living is both actually and normatively part of young people's lives today in stark contrast to earlier historical periods.

Before we make too much of this demographic trend, it is important to ask whether it really matters. From an institutional perspective it certainly does matter. The growing tendency to live independently is part of a number of trends signaling a decline in the significance of family life in

America. As others have noted, "rising ages at marriage, falling proportions of the population ever marrying, declining fertility and particularly
marital fertility, the sizeable proportion of marriages expected to end in
divorce, and the large numbers of children living with only one parent for
at least part of their childhood"—all trends that have accelerated
recently—can be seen as a further extension of the changes accompany-
ing modernization that have resulted in a decline in the centrality of the
family" (Waite, Goldscheider, and Witsberger, 1986:541).

From the perspective of the individual there are well-documented and
long-lasting consequences as well. Premarital independent living may
foster values and beliefs in opposition to traditional family structures.
From an analysis of a nationally representative longitudinal study that
followed over 10,000 14 to 24 year olds from 1968 until they were 10 years
older (in 1978), it was shown that the longer females live independently,
the more they change their plans for later work, their family size expectations, their attitude toward work by mothers, and their family-related sex-
role attitudes away from a traditional family orientation" (Waite et al.,
1986, 545). These young men and women became more individualistic in
their attitudes and aspirations as a consequence of living outside of
families. When these researchers speculated on *why* independent living
might have such effects, they offered the following:

> We suggest the following possibilities: First, living away from home
> lessens parental control over their children's activities and may
> weaken the link between parents' values, attitudes and behavior
> and those of their children. Young adults in their own apartments
> are freed from parental curfews and supervision of their friends and
> can manage their own household in the way that they choose. . . .
> (and) Living away from home may give both young men and
> women the self-confidence that they can get along without a family
> and may enable them to acquire the skills that they need to maintain
> their independence as long as they wish. (Waite et al., 1986:552).

Indeed, it is exactly the freedom from parental control that is of central
importance here. Without any significant others in the household, there is
immensely greater freedom, or emancipation.

The fact that this stage of the life course is historically unique is not
surprising. It is hard to imagine such an arrangement in earlier times. The
family (or family surrogate)has always served as a primary source of
social control. Parents are held accountable for the actions of their children; husbands have traditionally been held accountable for the actions of
their wives. No known society has structured living arrangements that
permit large numbers to be unattached to others. Living arrangements

serve very importantly to limit deviance by monitoring behaviors. Colonial American family structures illustrate this point clearly. In the absence of a state-sponsored police force, "The head of the household was charged with the duty of surveillance over the behaviors of everyone—of ruling the home with an iron hand and an all-seeing eye. This was the prevailing theory of family government" (Flaherty, 1972:56). Historically, the family served as the primary agent of social control in society.

I now turn to a brief summary of nest leaving and related phenomena since 1800.

Early Nineteenth to Early Twentieth Century

Soon after entering their teen years (around age 13 or 14) most youths in the early 1800s joined social institutions established by *adults* for youth. The variety of such organizations was immense; church groups, quasimilitary (militia), and self-improvement societies (abstinence clubs) existed side-by-side with junior versions of adult organizations (volunteer fire companies, for example). All such organizations were youth oriented, but adult sponsored and monitored.

Religious "conversion" was a very conspicuous youth activity that exposed youths to adult supervision and concurrently established reputations. Early in their teen years, youths would often accept, with obvious emotional conviction, the tenets of their parents' faith. This "conversion" was done in front of the entire assembled congregation of the church. According to Kett (1977:80,85), "The community bestowed visible marks of approval on a convert, for example, admitting him or her to full church membership. . . . Throughout the 19th century, no group surpassed evangelical Protestants in their institutional and intellectual concerns with youth."

The final leaving home usually came in the late teens or early twenties. Men often left home to migrate to cities where they would establish households with a spouse or live unmarried with relatives. For those who did neither, boarding houses offered family-like settings where a young man would live with others in the same line of work under the roof of a family home. There was virtually no independent living.

During the latter half of the nineteenth century, the growth of cities and population, the dramatic influx of immigrants, and continuing rapid industrialization, led to growing concerns over declining morality. During this historical era, we see the emergence of a belief that the "internalization of moral restraints and the formation of character were more likely to succeed in planned engineered environments than in casual ones" (Kett, 1977:112). The lives of young people, it was felt, should be more closely and regularly regimented. The inculcation of strong character (the source of guilt) was deemed essential and implied a need to control the total environment of the child.

This is understandable in light of the "new" view of childhood that emerged in the latter part of the century. Youthful experiences were coming, for the first time, to be viewed as formative. Young people, once treated as small adults, were now viewed as warranting special consideration because their early experiences were believed to influence their adult personalities. Age, as such, came to be a justification for differential treatment. Once this idea was accepted, age stratification became part of youth organizations; Sunday schools segregated youths by age, as did grammar schools. School years were lengthened from weeks to months and schooling made mandatory (from 1850 onward).

Where it had once been critical that a young person be "saved" (i.e., that they profess their religious conversion), cities made reputation more a matter of comportment, demeanor, manners, and attitudes. "Among the commercial classes of rapidly growing cities, a good name, unblemished morals, and steady behavior could have direct and practical values. Where *strangers* met and transacted business, outward demeanor was important to gain confidence but whether a man had finally made certain of his possession of "saving grace" mattered little (Kett, 1977:121, emphasis added).

It is especially important to note the consequence of growing urbanization and concentration of populations. In such settings, it was possible to be a stranger—to have no ascriptive reputation. This new category of individuals, those without recognized ties to others in the community, was responsible for the emergence of a new form of social control.

> In place of external regulation of conduct by village elders, ministers, or town officials, mid 19th century moralists substituted the cultivation of character in the regulated environment of family and school . . . The growth in cities, increase in population mobility, and rise of egalitarianism combined with evidence of social disorder, all contributed to the conviction that moral development of the young should no longer be shaped by casual contacts with adults in unstructured situations, but had to be regulated at every turn. (Kett, 1977:125–126)

The triumph of the idea of "development" (that the human personality developed in a cumulative fashion) meant that there were distinct, qualitatively different age categories. The one that was the most revolutionary, of course, was that of "adolescence"—a hitherto vague and rarely used term. The teen years assumed great importance within this new view of human development. To control and structure experiences during this dangerous period of development required that the young person remain in their parents' household. Indeed, attendance at Academies, the practice of apprenticeship and "putting out" declined during the second half of the nineteenth century. Youth, it was felt, should remain in their parents' homes, should be monitored, and should be subject to rigid structured experiences—in schools and in their families. Again, this emphasis on parental control sprang forth with the growth of populations and migration. The loss of easily known reputation and the inability to monitor fostered new and structured methods of controlling behavior; a shift from relying on shame to relying on the inculcation of guilt as the mechanism for controlling behaviors had begun.

Industrialization and immigration, and all their associated social consequences, also fostered a changed view of youth. Where apprenticeship had once been necessary for the acquisition of virtually any skilled avocation, machinery made long apprenticeships unnecessary. Those who would work in industry needed little training. Those who aspired to the professions, however, did. Educational credentials emerged for the first time. On completing a course of study, an individual was awarded some form of credential, or diploma. The University of Virginia, founded in 1819, did not award degrees until 1848. After completing a course of study, a student received a certificate of completion. Actual *degrees* (e.g., the Bachelor of Arts) were awarded only after 1848. Among strangers, a diploma was a formal introduction—a credential that certified certain traits deemed essential but otherwise unknowable. Credentials, in short, established reputations among strangers. Between 1890 and 1920 many professions established, for the first time, formal standards for eligibility. For the practice of law, medicine, pharmacy, dentistry, or veterinary medicine, one would now be required to obtain the relevant diploma or attend the specialized school. Without such certification, how could anyone know whether the practitioner was competent? Without easily known reputations, how could one know who to trust?

The late nineteenth and early twentieth century in America was an era of rapidly expanding certification requirements in many fields. Then, as now, such certification was tied less directly to the substantive requirements for proficiency in a field than to the larger social problem of a diverse population of strangers. How was one to know if a physician was competent? Unlike physicians in Europe who had a longstanding tradition of guilds that could exercise control over which doctors were permitted to practice, American physicians for most of the nineteenth century were not governed by any formal requirements to practice their craft. The establishment of licensing requirements and professional schools distinguished "regular" (trained and certified) physicians from "folk" doctors. Was there any real difference in their respective success rates or the likelihood of cures? Perhaps, but only minimally so. Licensing and certification professionalized the practice of medicine. From the perspective of physicians this was clearly a good thing. From the perspective of patients, it was also minimal assurance that one's doctor was bound by accepted conventions, was knowledgeable about whatever "modern" medicine offered, and could be trusted to abide by certain standards. The license on the wall was all the reputation a doctor needed to open a practice. It was all the patient needed to subject himself to the ministrations of the doctor.

What worked for the professional classes also worked for those at lower class levels. A degree from a high school increasingly became important for success. The high-school diploma served the same purpose the medical license did—it established an individual's claims to certain traits, skills, and attitudes. For it to do so, secondary schools assumed greater and greater control over the lives of their charges. As did their college counterparts, most students in high school participated in numerous extracurricular organizations, thereby extending the authority of the school more widely.

Credentials, certificates, and licenses were responses to fears and concerns over the uncertainties inherent in larger and denser cities, of immigrant groups with strange and unfamiliar moral standards, of heterogeneity, of strangers. In cities, youths had new opportunities for unsupervised activities. In movie houses, youths mixed in heterosexual groups totally unsupervised by adults—an unprecedented possibility. Automobiles, similarly, altered the supervision abilities of adults. And such lack of supervision was blamed for all manner of deviance. The idea that youths might get into trouble if left on their own fostered an entirely new concept in the early 1900s; juvenile delinquency. The delinquent was viewed as an otherwise ordinary young person who had not been sufficiently supervised by parents. All young persons were viewed as potential delinquents—and thus in need of close monitoring.

The increasing importance placed on regular and structured education of youths is reflected in employment statistics for the early twentieth century. In 1910, half of all American boys of 15 had been gainfully employed. By 1930, that proportion was down to only one-sixth (Modell, 1989:79). A similar trend was observed among young girls—from one in four to one in twelve. As historian John Modell argues, these pronounced changes reflect a fundamental change in family economies: "The age at which children would begin 'paying back' their parents for the investments they had made in them was postponed over this period for two years or longer, the greater part of this change coming in the 1920s" (Modell, 1989:79).

The life course of youths became more and more structured in concert with the growing insistence on controlling young peoples' experiences. Limited more and more to their roles as high school students, young people found new outlets for their free time. Dance halls and movie palaces were popular forms of adolescent recreation in the early twentieth century. "Between 1921 and 1930, average weekly attendance at motion pictures increased rapidly. A weekly movie habit, or more, was typical of unmarried youth, who characteristically attended with age-peers" (Modell, 1989:73). This form of recreation quickly supplanted the older type of mate selection—courtship. Dating, an entirely new form of casual mixed-sex relationship, grew to prominence in the 1920s.

Dating is significant as an historically unique form of mate selection in the west. It stressed physical attractiveness, thrills, and competition above the more traditional concerns over family name and homogamous economic position. Most importantly, dating, unlike courtship, was peer supervised. A date took place *away* from home and unchaperoned by parents. Comparing the older custom of courtship to the newly emerging pattern of dating, Modell (1989:88) noted:

> Under the older system there was no normatively sanctioned way for an adolescent to get "serious" about someone of the opposite sex without submitting the relationship for parental approval. Chaperonage asserted parents' oversight of what boys and girls might do together, and the home visit assured girls' parents of some control over whom their daughters might be seeing. Both were important, and both vanished with dating, which substituted peer oversight. Not the occurrence of emotional or physical intimacy but the question of whose advice guided young people in developing heterosexual ties was the critical difference between dating and the practice of "calling" and "keeping company" that it was rapidly supplanting in the 1920s.

As Modell notes, it was not the automobile or other forms of transportation (public streetcars, for example) that were crucial for the emergence of dating. Rather, it was the availability of somewhere to go to that was acceptable to a girl's parents that mattered. That dating emerged first in cities rather than rural areas attests to the importance of legitimate (acceptable) forms of recreation away from home, like movies and dance halls.

Dating assumes even greater significance when its impact on parental influence and control is considered. The "rules" of courtship had been the province of the girl's parents. And even though dating may not have appeared as an alternative to courtship, that is what it became. The patterns of heterosexual recreation established a stable system of matching individuals as mates that was governed by clear standards of conduct. But unlike courtship, the system of dating was more or less immune from direct parental involvement. Noting that dating emerged first among middle-class whites (though the custom quickly spread down the social class ladder and across racial lines) Modell (1989:92) observed:

> the fully evolved date itself had a compelling logic quite distinct from that of prior forms of courtship: it was a step in an ongoing negotiation, with rules defined and deviations punished by age peers. The logic of the date anchored it in modest pleasures and centered the choices it occasioned in the daters themselves (within limits imposed by the peer culture). The home visit or chaperoned dance, in essence, had been either purely sociable—part of a group occasion—or explicitly related to courtship. The date might turn out to be either of these, or both, or most commonly, something else again, but what it turned out to be depended on how well the negotiation at its core went, a negotiation regarding short-term gratification.

Those short-term gratifications (or thrills) typically included healthy doses of sexual excitement, or "petting." Yet even a practice so obviously threatening to traditional values of female chastity was consistent with more general attitudes concerning adolescent development. Sexual experimentation short of intercourse was seen as part of "normal" adolescent development. Dating liberated women much more so than it did men. It was the girl's father's responsibility to safeguard her virtue in earlier times. Her behaviors were subject to considerably greater scrutiny than were her suitor's. The young male was required to proffer a good reputation when he came calling—an established name justifying his proper intentions and deserving the trust of his intended's father. But the young woman was expected to avoid all untoward advances such a young man might make. In dating, by contrast, the double standard was explicitly challenged. But it was not overthrown.

The peer culture ensured that girls not be too liberal in their sexual favors. The young woman who was too quick to respond with sexual favors lost her good reputation among her peers. Boys, however, suffered no such loss of good name for their sexual exploits. Still, dating was governed by well-known standards of behavior despite some disagreement between boys and girls over the "allowable" freedom to be expected in sexual matters. The tension for girls was to balance the popular requirement to be a desired date against the negative consequences of being labeled "easy."

The peer regulation of dating was firmly incorporated in the high school culture by the mid-1920s. Through various symbols and actions, young students demonstrated their accession to the rules of the game. Girls wore boys' club pins to demonstrate something more than a casual dating relationship with a boy. Clothing, similarly, distinguished those who were "desirable" as dates. High school dances, a very popular form of recreation, allowed boys and girls to demonstrate to their peers their dating successes. "Beyond visible symbols, word of mouth was powerful where everybody was likely to know everybody. . . . Gossip, of course, regulated behavior. [and] Chiding served to educate boys to the proper ways of behaving toward girls, so that the rules of the dating system might be learned even by the more backward among them" (Modell, 1989:102).

In the course of two decades, between the turn of the century and the end of the 1920s, the life course of youths had been significantly altered. A stable parent-run system of courtship had largely given way to a stable participant-run system of dating. Casual heterosexual pairing was accepted as a normal part of growing up—an unexceptional element of adolescent development. Most importantly, parental supervision and surveillance of their children were now partially replaced by peer-culture norms. Dating imposed strong pressures on youths to conform to widely shared standards of propriety. A young person's reputation depended largely on his or her success in the dating market. . . on how they "rated" as dates. Not parental sanctions, but the specter of peer shame now operated to encourage conformity.

The Great Depression

The extent to which these changes in the lives of young people were a result of economic forces can be gauged by considering the consequences of the Great Depression of the 1930s. Among those families hurt by the Depression, those who experienced unemployment or declines in economic well-being, the areas of consumption most immediately affected were those directly tied to the new freedoms that youths had come to take for granted. Recreation, automobiles, and fashionable clothing were sacrificed to the hard economic times. A decade before, "families were using a relatively substantial portion of their prosperity to adorn their late-adolescent sons and daughters, as these children neared marriageable age in the new marriage market that was beginning to incorporate dating" (Modell, 1989:130). The two central symbolic pillars of dating; fashionable clothing and commercial entertainment (movies or dances), appear to have been the areas parents were most willing to economize on. After all, these parents had grown up in an era in which dating was, at least, less common and for most, nonexistent.

The hardships in securing employment also meant that it was more difficult for young people to strike out on their own to establish a new family. First marriages were delayed, on average, by about a year during the early 1930s. Since marriages followed from dating, one might think such a trend indicated substantial changes in this institution. While dating may have been less focused on material symbolism than it had a decade earlier, there is little evidence that the most important consequence of dating—mating—was significantly altered during the Depression. In fact, dating remained essentially unchanged during the decade. But the institution of dating as a prelude to marriage was problematic precisely because of its transient and unstable nature.

Intervening between dating and marriage was the stage of engagement. No longer for "thrills," the relationship during an engagement period was a more serious stage in the family-formation process lasting, on average, 6 months to a year. Engaged couples occupied a different status than dating couples. Once their intentions to marry were made public, a couple was subject to different norms governing their behaviors. Most particularly, greater sexual freedoms were customary in engagement. Coitus, however, had not customarily been expected during this stage of family formation. During the Depression, however, such restraints began to weaken.

With the traditional route to marriage (courtship) no longer common, engagement served to bridge the institutions of dating and marriage. And just as dating was governed by strong peer standards, so too engagement expanded the discretion exercised by the young couple themselves in negotiating their relationship. During the decade, engagements tended to be shorter than they had been in the prior decade. But the more significant change was the growing tolerance for sexual intimacy. Part of this change can be traced to the economic obstacles faced by those wishing to marry. Longer delays before marriage were countered by greater unwillingness to forego sex during that interval. So, while engagement, itself, underwent no profound changes in the 1930s, the content of the status did; couples exercised greater sexual freedom. And in so doing, individual prerogative increased, parental control declined.

World War II

World War II had its effects on the life course of young people primarily through the economic changes it caused. Where employment problems had the effect, during the Depression, of lengthening the years spent in school, the sharp rise in demand for industrial workers during the war had the opposite effect. Those who wished to could leave high school and find work. And even those who did not drop out of high school could find part-time work to finance their dating and recreation. In one sense, the war eliminated many of the effects of the Depression. A Census Bureau sample survey in April 1944 indicated that over one in five of schoolboys 14 to 16 were gainfully employed, and over two in five at 16 to 17. "By this time, 35 percent had left school altogether and were work-ing. . . . The twentieth century trend toward an extended period of eco-nomic dependency, based on school extension and exclusion from the full-time labor force, had been reversed momentarily" (Modell, 1989:166).

In fact, the war had very few measurable effects on aggregate measures of family formation. Indeed, marriage rates and age-at-first marriage figures show little, if any, demonstrable consequence of the war. Even with large numbers of young males on active duty, dating and marriage weathered the times largely unaffected. Modell speculates that one reason for this was the existence of a double standard of sexual conduct that granted men great license while away from home while, at the same time, admonishing such men's wives and fiancees to both understand the unusual circumstances surrounding such actions and to comport them-selves in the most proper ways. In short, the licentious behaviors of soldiers was understood as a justifiable consequence of the unusual situation of wartime (Modell, 1989:198–200).

The Baby Boom

The true "effect" of World War II appeared only after it was over. The very healthy postwar economy and the independence and assurance gained by young people during the War combined to foster new and unusual patterns of negotiating the life course. The early marriages and high fertility of the postwar cohort of young adults are well-known, despite the lack of accepted explanations for them. But there is little doubt that the postwar economy had much to do with the possibilities of pursuing early marriage and childbearing.

A number of attitudinal and financial indicators attest to the optimism of consumers during the late 1940s and 1950s. Growing proportions of Americans expressed the opinion that they were better off than they had been the previous year (Board of Governors of the Federal Reserve System, 1949). There was a dramatic increase in the use of borrowing to finance consumer items and homes (Board of Governors of the Federal Reserve System, 1957). Mortgage assistance for GIs and the building of new suburban housing contributed to rapid growth in home ownership.

Part of the economic prosperity of the Baby Boom era was bought with additional earners in the family. Women had supported the war effort in industry only to be the first laid off after armistice. However, during the 1950s, women's labor force participation rates recovered to near what

they had been during the previously unprecedented wartime rates. Between 1940 and 1945 the female labor force expanded dramatically from
28.9 to 38.1 percent of the female population. By 1947, however, this
percentage had dropped to 30.8 percent. By 1955, 35.7 percent of women
were in the labor force. By 1960, 37.7 percent were. These changes in
participation rates are a reflection of a change in the type of woman who
worked. During the war, the typical female worker was young and single,
the peak participation rate being for women 20 to 24 years old. The
women who entered the labor force after the war, however, were increasingly married and older. By 1960, the percentage of women over 34 who
were in the labor force rose dramatically, with the largest increase in the
45 to 54 age group. (U.S. Department of Labor, 1969). Between 1948 and
1960, the proportion of wives with no children under 18 who worked rose
only 3 percentage points (from 28 to 31 percent) whereas the comparable
figures for women with school-aged children (6 to 18) rose fifteen points
(from 21 to 36 percent).

The increase in married mothers' labor force participation is of tremendous significance for the monitoring and supervising of children. Given
the tendency for older mothers to work, supervision of adolescents by
mothers declined. The changing nature of parental supervision was sin-
gled out as one of several important causes of juvenile delinquency—a
phenomenon that attracted great attention in the early 1950s. In fact,
youth, as a category, attracted considerable concern during the decade. As
Modell (1989:233) summarizes:

> A generalized concern over juvenile delinquency evokes the sense
> of ill-chosen innovation. . . which haunted the period. Not very
> deep below the surface lay the fear of a youth culture with distinc-
> tive values—about the restraint of impulse and sexuality more
> particularly—and a deep resentment of that portion of adult com-
> mercial culture that pandered directly to the developing distinctive
> tastes of youth.

That youths had embarked on self-governed patterns of dating and sex
was widely accepted in the 1950s albeit with generalized concern and fear
for the consequences. Youthful sexual license aroused great anxiety
among parents as it had in all prior generations. However, unlike prior
generations this one seemed much more liberal in their sexual attitudes
and behaviors.

The absolute number of young people in schools during the Baby Boom
also had consequences for monitoring of behaviors. Between 1946 and
1960, the average number of students per public secondary school increased by nearly one-half (Modell, 1989:225). Within their high schools,

unprecedented numbers of youths were mixed together. The variety of backgrounds and interests of these youths of similar ages found expression in the diversity of youth organizations and cliques that formed. And a youth culture emerged—a widely accepted pattern of behaviors, beliefs, and appearance. Central to this culture was the universal (among youth) custom of dating. The children of the Baby Boom were offspring of parents who, themselves, understood dating. For these parents, dating thus was not a novel institution. Instead, it was well known and understood by parents and children alike. What the parents of these children had fought over with *their* parents was now generally viewed as normal, adolescent development. Dating had triumphed as a ubiquitous part of being a teenager. As James Coleman's research on high-school students revealed, popularity among students was directly tied to *peer-established* criteria: athletic prowess and attractiveness (Coleman, 1971) Students segregated themselves into numerous cliques, ranked by their restrictiveness. Certain groups were comprised of the most popular students; others were comprised of the "brains," and so on.

The importance of the youth culture is that it completed the trend established in the 1920s. By 1960, students, *themselves* established the standards by which dating and mate selection proceeded. Within the high school one found the mechanism for sorting partners—a mechanism that was established and maintained by the students, not their parents or teachers.

Dating began around the time one began high school (age 15) and by 11th grade, virtually all students had begun dating. In his tabulations from a national sample of 4,000 students interviewed as part of Project Talent, Modell found that in 1960 over 96 percent of all urban white-collar and blue-collar males and females had begun dating by that grade. Marginally smaller percentages of farm students had dated by then (Modell, 1989:Table 29).

While the parents of the Baby Boom knew, understood, and approved of dating, there was much less consensus over "going steady"—a more serious form of commitment in which couples limited their dating to only each other. Much as their parents had feared the autonomy offered by dating, parents of the Baby Boom generation expressed similar concerns over going steady. This stage in relationships was increasingly popular among students in the 1950s. A steady relationship promised greater and greater intimacies, something understood by both parents and children. Furthermore, going steady removed some of the competitiveness from dating. Once selected, a steady girlfriend posed little risk to a young man who might, otherwise, face ridicule for being denied a date. Where their parents had dated for popularity in the 1930s, youths in the 1950s went

steady for more emotionally personal reasons—often after an open pro-
fession of deep love.

Greater emotional commitments at earlier ages permitted (though
probably did not cause) a significant drop in the age at first marriage.
Median ages at first marriage were 24.3 and 21.5 (males and females,
respectively) in 1940 but only 22.6 and 20.2 in 1955 (U.S. Bureau of the
Census, 1979). Coupled with an increase of about 1 year in the age at
which young people left school, "The transition time to adulthood was
thus compressed sharply in the baby boom decade" (Modell, 1989:251).

The 1970s and 1980s

The single best clue to how dating and premarital relationships
changed after the Baby Boom is how marriage is viewed. The past two
decades have seen a growing sense that marriage is an impediment to
autonomy—something that one postpones until ready to sacrifice that
freedom. Marriage is now viewed as a forum for personal fulfillment, not
for sacrifice. The cultural forces that led to this are numerous. But the
challenges by youths to authority so well-documented for the decade of
the 1960s may be viewed as part of the quest for autonomy and freedom
from conventional restraints. The feminist critique sought to "liberate"
women. And in general, the political and social climate among youths in
the 1970s and 1980s was consistent in asserting autonomy and freedom
from convention; marital roles, sexual norms, and gender roles were all
questioned. Marriages were postponed, sex and cohabitation before marriage were not. Fertility declined as birth control, divorce, and personal
autonomy increased.

The custom of dating died, or was at least mortally wounded, in the
late 1960s and early 1970s. Challenges to gender roles were part of the
reason. Dating was an asymmetrical form of male–female relationship. It
required a more-or-less formalized pattern of reciprocity, initiated by the
male and responded to by the female. The formality of dating and the
rigid structures it imposed on relationships were rejected by the younger
generation. In short, the normative regulation of behavior by *peers* was
less acceptable. In the place of dating, more casual, mixed-sex group
activities became popular. "Hanging out" replaced dating. Girls could
initiate a pairing up, as could boys. But there was much less structure
imposed on relationships by youthful peers. Indeed, there was much less
pressure to go out at all. Where a generation before dating had been
essential for any level of popularity, in the 1970s and 1980s, this was
certainly not so. Where frequency of contact with the opposite sex had
once depended on parental decision, later on peer pressure, it was now

individual preference. Social control of heterosexual relationships had moved from parents, to peers, to partners.

The relative absence of parental or peer control among youths meant that relationships were negotiated one-on-one with less direct influence from others. As a result, there was greater variability among couples in what they viewed as acceptable, what they aspired to, and how they conducted their relationships. Attitudes about premarital sex, for example, revealed much less consensus (greater variance) in the 1970s than they had in the 1950s or 1960s (Modell, 1989:Table 49).

The individualization of youth corresponds to a growing emphasis on personality and freedom. Yet, while youths are less controlled directly by adults (in their schools or other aspects of life), they are, as Modell (1989:326) concludes, "increasingly dependent on certification from formal institutions controlled by adults and find themselves entangled in bureaucratic career lines of frustratingly gradual ascent." Indeed, the centrality of certification and other methods of establishing a reputation are not the least bit curious. They are the methods of social control that have replaced or augmented parents and peers.

Trends in Emancipation: Statistics from 1947 to the Present

Every year since 1947 the U.S. Bureau of the Census has conducted yearly national surveys that are used to measure the marital status and living arrangements of adults and children. For each year since 1947 I have calculated the percentage of males and females aged 20 to 24 and aged 25 to 29 who do not live in a family. A family is defined in conventional terms: two or more persons residing together, and related by birth, marriage, or adoption. A person who does not live in a family may be living alone or may share a residence with others to whom he or she is not related. Cohabiting couples, by the Census Bureau definition, would not be families. Students at college are counted as living in their parents', not their own domiciles. For that reason, residents of dormitories or apartments who are attending college but who are still counted as dependents of their parents are not enumerated as living outside of a family. This means that an increase or decrease in the number of college students (many of whom do not live at home) will have no measurable effect on the estimates of emancipation I am using (Figure 1).

Several trends are immediately apparent. First, the largest increase in emancipation has occurred since the early 1970s. It was in 1973 that the

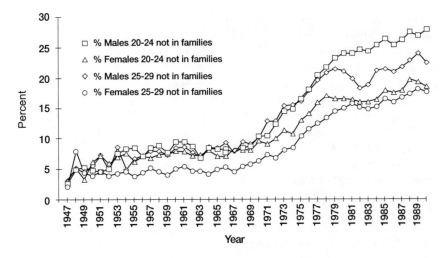

Figure 1. Trends in emancipation: 1947–1990.

Notes: For 1947, Family Status was determined by whether the respondent was "in a household." Also, values for ages 20–24 were estimated from totals for 18–24 year olds. Similar procedures were used for the 25–29 age group by using the 25–34 figures. The original publication included age categories of 18–24 and 25–34.

*For 1948, the percentage "in families" was not produced separately by sex and age. Plotted values were estimated by applying the total percentage not in families for each age group (not by sex) to male and female totals (assuming equal percentages for both males and females of each age).

*For 1949, figures for ages 25–29 are estimated from the 25–34 age bracket. The percent in families is estimated (for 20–24 year olds) using the percent of 14–24 year olds in families. For the 25–29 age group, the published percentage of 25–44 year olds was used.

*For 1951, "Not in Families" meant "Unrelated Individual." The percent in families is the same for males and females for this year (see note for 1948 above).

Source: U.S. Bureau of the Census, Current Population Reports, Series P-20. For 1947–1950, figures are from various CPS reports on Marital Status. For 1950–1970, figures are from *Marital Status and Family Status* reports. For 1971–1991, figures are from *Marital Status and Living Arrangement* reports.

See Appendices A and B for figures used in all graphs.

twenty-sixth Amendment to the Constitution was passed enfranchising 18 to 20 year olds. And most states lowered their legal ages of majority during the 1970s. It would appear that actual emancipation (i.e., actually living on one's own) was clearly on the rise before the legal ratification of that practice (i.e., eliminating the disabilities of minority age for those 18 to 21). Between 1947 and 1970, the percentage of emancipated persons aged 20 to 29 increased from between 2 and 3 percent to between 6 and 9 percent. But from 1970 to 1990 it increased much more—from between 6 and 9 percent to between 18 and 24 percent of persons aged 20 to 29. So, while the rates of emancipation have been increasing for both males and females since at least 1947, the most notable and pronounced increases occurred since the early 1970s.

For both sexes, a major factor in the increasing rates of nonfamily living is the later and later age at first marriage. In 1947, median ages at first marriage were 23.7 for men and 20.5 for women. By 1990 the corresponding figures had increased to 26.1 (males) and 23.9 (females). (U.S. Bureau of the Census. 1991a: Table A). People who postpone getting married either continue to live at home or strike out on their own. These figures confirm what casual observation suggests: more and more young people are leaving home to live independently of either parents or spouse.

The second trend apparent in the graph is the higher rates of emancipation for males than for females, especially since the 1970s. Looking at those 20 to 24, three percent of males and three percent of females were emancipated in 1947. In 1957 the comparable figures were again equal: 7 percent. By 1967, however, 9 percent of males, but 7 percent of females this age were living outside of families. Larger differences emerge as one follows the trends through the 1970s. By 1977 18 percent of males but only 14 percent of females were emancipated. And in 1990 the difference was five percentage points (24 percent of males and 19 percent of females emancipated). For males and females 25 to 29, male–female differences are more apparent for all historical periods. In 1957, 4 percent of females 25 to 29 lived outside of families compared to 7 percent of males. By 1990 the corresponding figures were 18 and 27 percent.

Females marry at younger ages than males. As a result, for any age group under 30, a higher proportion of males will be unmarried. In fact, prior to the early 1970s most states set a lower age of majority for females than for males. The distinction was based on females' earlier maturity and on the prevailing view about their proper social role; in the home, not the marketplace. The U.S. Supreme Court declared such distinctions unconstitutional in 1971 and 1975 [*Reed v. Reed*, 404 U.S. 71 75 (1971); *Stanton v. Stanton*, 421 U.S. 7 (1975)].

Males at all ages have higher rates of employment and higher wages than females. Since employment is necessary for most people who wish to live independently, males have been more able to financially support themselves than females.

Finally it should be noted that older (25 to 29) people have marginally different rates of emancipation than their younger (20 to 24) counterparts. In general, older females are less likely to live outside of families than younger females. Among females in 1970, for example, 8 percent of 20 to 24 year olds were emancipated compared with 6 percent of 25 to 29 year olds. In 1990 a similar difference is noted; 19 percent of 20- to 24-year-old females and 18 percent of 25- to 29-year-old females lived outside of families. Among males, the opposite is true. Older males are slightly more likely to live in nonfamily households than are younger males. In 1990 24 percent of the younger and 27 percent of the older group lived outside of families.

I have discussed many forces that contributed to these demographic trends. It is the consequences or corollaries of the growth in non-family living that is the next topic to be discussed.

The history of emancipation of youth is also the history of significant changes in individual autonomy. By virtue of their non-family living arrangements and many other legal and social changes (e.g., dating customs, statutory emancipation, lowered age of majority) young people are less constrained by traditional sources of control. In one very real sense, the family is less central to the lives of young adults because they have been emancipated from some of the routine influence and constraint once imposed by resident kin. Whether one reads this history as evidence of greater individual autonomy or of diminished family influence, the conclusion is the same: youths have greater autonomy in decisions about their lives than they did in the past. This autonomy is part of what I have described as personal privacy. Legitimate immunity from others' scrutiny, that is, implies some degree of legitimate immunity from others' direct influence and control.

The greater privacy and autonomy enjoyed by youths has contributed to the development and elaboration of various forms of social control. As I noted earlier, it is not necessarily true that unsupervised youths *are* a threat to conventional legal and moral standards. Indeed, that is an empirical question that warrants serious investigation. Rather, it is the perception that emancipated youths might not be trustworthy that matters. If it is believed that the absence of traditional mechanisms of monitoring and control fosters deviance, then those who might suffer as a result will seek new ways to safeguard against it. Any such social structure will be directed at the autonomous individual. In the next two chapters I discuss the increase in surveillance that has accompanied the increase in emancipation of young adults. Overt surveillance in the form of credentials and ordeals is directed at autonomous individuals. Surveillance of this sort counterbalances some of the individual autonomy and privacy that individuals enjoy. These costs of privacy are best seen as part of the inherent tensions between individual autonomy and collective order. It is that tension that I hope to capture in my description of surveillance as a cost that is incurred for privacy.

3

CREDENTIALS

Introduction

The ordinary life of modern Americans is full of strangers. When we discover that we are suffering from some malady, we seek the advice and care of a specialist. But how do we know that this individual's advice can be trusted? When we purchase major items such as automobiles or homes, we ordinarIly ask a financial institution to extend credit. But how can the lender determine whether or not our repayment pledge should be honored? Young college graduates apply for jobs in various distant places. But how can an employer ascertain whether the technically qualified applicant is trustworthy? How, when so many people we deal with are strangers, do we demonstrate our own trustworthiness or establish theirs?

There is certainly nothing new about this dilemma. Human communities of modest size have always contained more people than permitted universal recognition. It is difficult to imagine modern societies where everyone knows everyone else well. Undoubtedly there were once small intimate societies that permitted such familiarity. But such societies are extremely rare today. It is the size and complexity of communities that make trust so very difficult.

In small groupings, there is little about others that cannot be, or is not, known. The comings and goings of settlers of early American communities were conspicuous and the modern value of privacy virtually unknown. In the absence of widespread privacy, it is a relatively easy thing to know whether or not someone is trustworthy. As sociologist Georg Simmel noted almost a century ago:

> In very simple circumstances the lie is more harmless in regard to the maintenance of the group than under more complex conditions. Primitive man who lives in a small group, who satisfies his needs through his own production or through direct cooperation, who

43

limits his intellectual interests to his own experiences or to unilinear tradition, surveys and controls the material of his life more easily and completely than does the man of higher cultures. To be sure, the innumerable errors and superstitions in the life of primitive man are harmful enough to him, but far less so than are corresponding ones in advanced epochs, because the practice of his life is guided in the main by those few facts and circumstances of which his narrow range of vision permits him to gain directly a *correct* view. In a richer and larger cultural life, however, existence rests on a thousand premises which the single individual cannot trace and verify to their roots at all, but must take on faith. Our modern life is based to a much larger extent than is usually realized upon the faith in the honesty of the other. . . . *We base our gravest decisions on a complex system of conceptions, most of which presuppose the confidence that we will not be betrayed.* Under modern conditions, the lie, therefore, becomes something much more devastating than it was earlier, something which questions the very foundations of our life. (Simmel, in Wolfe, 1950 :313. emphasis added).

Just as parents know whether or not the claims made by their 6-year-old child are true, so the members of intimate communities could recognize a lie rather easily. The dilemma one faces when a stranger's child makes a claim (is it true?) is a metaphor for the more general problem we all face in a complex society. How can we know if what another says is or is not true?

Trust depends on the faith we have in another person's truthfulness. Why, for example, are we more willing to trust a doctor we have never consulted before than a car salesman we do not know? Why are the criticisms of a college professor taken more seriously than those of a high-school drop-out? The answer to such questions is that we trust those whose *reputations* justify our trust. It is reputation that earns trust and it is a lack of reputation that produces doubt and skepticism.

Surveillance, as I use that word, is how reputations may be established and maintained. Since privacy (and the proliferation of strangers) is the reason others' reputations are not known, surveillance may be seen as the cost of privacy. It is possible to define certain domains of life as legitimately beyond the scrutiny of others—that is, to establish realms of privacy—because surveillance provides that which is lost to privacy, reputations.

Computerized systems that permit others to investigate our employment or financial background are gaining widespread popularity among employers and creditors. Although some may decry the establishment of computerized records of individuals as a "loss of privacy," it would be more correct to see such developments as the *cost* of vastly expanded amounts of privacy. Indeed, there would be little need for massive data bases on individuals were there no privacy. Simmel's observation about the irrelevance of the lie among intimates makes this point quite clearly. If we knew everything about everyone, there would be little reason to collect and store the details of their biographies. It is only because major portions of our everyday experiences are legitimately (often legally) defined as beyond scrutiny that distrust can arise. Is it, in other words, only because we enjoy such great privacy that surveillance arises in the first place. To enjoy some degree of predictable social order, we may have either privacy *and* surveillance, or have little privacy.

As I have already explained, reputations are increasingly established and maintained in two ways—through credentials and through ordeals. Surveillance, in other words, may be defined conceptually as consisting of these two operative components. In this chapter I consider credentials. Ordeals are discussed in the following chapter.

In an attempt to render the discussion of credentials manageable, I have selected only three types. A credential is defined as something that gives an individual access to credit or confidence. Therefore I will examine credit cards (a means of establishing title to credit), drivers' licenses (not only an entitlement to confidence, but also the most common form of identification), and educational credentials (a means of establishing trust and confidence). I selected these examples rather than professional credentials or licenses for the practice of trades because they are more generally available. That is, the potential population of those holding one or more of these credentials is greater than for any other combination of credentials. This permits limited empirical investigation of my central argument—that credentials are a function of privacy.

The empirical evidence consists of very simple relationships. I have established, for every year since 1947, the percentage of young people who are emancipated (i.e., not living in a family). These young people, I propose, lack easily known reputations to a greater degree than comparable youths living in their own or their parents' families. When the relative numbers of such youths increase or decrease (both of which have occurred since the end of World War II), there should be a corresponding increase or decrease in the percentage who hold various sorts of credentials. To the extent possible, I have established for the same years the relative numbers of youths who are licensed to drive, who hold credit cards, and who have various educational credentials.

When the percentage of emancipated youths in an historical era increases, we should observe an increase in the percentage of youths who hold credit cards, educational credentials, and drivers' licenses in the same general period. Such a relationship, if found, would support the central thesis of this book. Of course, it is always possible that some third factor might be responsible for simultaneous changes in both emancipation and credentials. Correlations of the sort I just described would not establish a causal relationship. It is undoubtedly true that rising affluence and commercial growth each foster increases in the use of credit and automobile drivers' licenses (and, perhaps, other types of credentials). Higher rates of college attendance are also a feature of greater affluence and economic growth. These trends are each part of my story. Whether emancipation (or, more generally, the rise of strangers and privacy) is independent of such large trends is not really at issue. I am not attempting to isolate *the* cause of changes in surveillance. Credentials are one form of surveillance. And surveillance is one response to rising numbers of strangers. That surveillance may have other causes and consequences (increasing numbers of drivers licenses *do* after all, reflect the fact that there are more and more people who are required to drive) is not at all inconsistent with my argument.

Before considering the historical evidence about the rise of credentials, it is helpful to briefly consider a time when strangers were not so conspicuous—when reputations might be established in more familiar, conventional ways. As I will develop later in this chapter, the massive waves of immigration near the turn of the twentieth century appear to be the immediate stimulus for unprecedented concerns over strangers. The late nineteenth and early twentieth century period was a watershed era for the rise of both privacy and credentials. Prior to that time, reputations depended on quite local standards of decorum—demonstrated in localities among one's associates. Such a pattern relied on little migration and frequent face-to-face contact. But rapid urbanization and migration associated with massive immigration made these traditional methods of establishing and maintaining reputations unworkable.

When Max Weber visited the United States in 1904, he commented on how traditional methods of maintaining reputations were being supplanted. Weber recounts several personal experiences to make his point.

A German-born nose and throat specialist, who had established himself in a large city on the Ohio River . . . told me of the visit of his first patient. Upon the doctor's request, he lay down upon the couch to be examined with the aid of a nose reflector. The patient sat up once and remarked with dignity and emphasis, "Sir, I am a member of the _____ Baptist Church in _____ Street." Puzzled about what meaning this circumstance might have for the disease of the nose and its treatment, the doctor discretely inquired about the matter from an American colleague. The colleague smilingly informed him that the patient's statement of his church membership was merely to say; "Don't worry about the fees." (Weber, 1958:304)

In rural North Carolina, Weber discovered that admission to a local Baptist congregation required the most rigorous inquiry into one's character and background going all the way back to childhood.

Admission to the congregation is recognized as an absolute guarantee of the moral qualities of a gentleman, especially of those qualities required in business matters. Baptism secures to the individual the deposits of the whole region and unlimited credit without any competition. In general, *only* those men had success in business who belonged to Methodist or Baptist or other *sects* or sectlike conventicles [religious assemblies]. When a sect member moved to a different place, or if he was a traveling salesman, he carried the certificate of his congregation with him; and thereby he found not only easy contact with sect members but, above all, he found credit everywhere. (Weber, 1958:305).

Credit-worthiness, Weber discovered, depended on the knowledge that a reputable religious sect would accept only those whose conduct made them appear to be morally qualified beyond doubt. Sect (congregation) membership, in short, established reputations. But church (denomination) membership did not. One was *born* into a church. One was *admitted* into a congregation—through baptism. "Today, the kind of denomination to which one belongs is rather irrelevant. What is decisive is that one be admitted to membership by 'ballot,' after an *examination*" (Weber, 1958:307).

What Weber discovered in backwoods North Carolina was not to be found in the urbanizing areas of the country at the turn of the century. By 1904, congregation membership could not count for much in the larger urban areas of America because of sheer size and density. Here (in cities) Weber observed the custom of wearing a "little badge" (what we today call a lapel pin) in the buttonhole that signified membership in some form of (usually) secular association. Membership in such organizations as the Masons required an examination and a ballot. Weber described the emergence of such organizations as the "secularization" of American society as they replaced religious sects in larger areas. The interpretation given to the lapel pin custom by Weber was that these badges were used for reputational purposes. "The badge in the buttonhole meant, 'I am a gentleman patented after investigation and approbation and guaranteed by my membership'" (Weber, 1958:308).

Reputation at the turn of this century, at least to the extent needed to conduct business, depended on *admission* to a sect, club, fraternal society, or other organization that was recognized as legitimate. Such member-ship, displayed with a pin in the lapel or however else, was a credential that could be traded on to justify others trust or credit.

The reputation-conferring function of religious denominations dated from the earliest colonists—especially the Puritans. This was especially so in the larger communities of New England. But by 1904, the reputational component of religious congregations had diminished considerably and secular counterparts were in abundance to perform the same task. Un-doubtedly, voluntary associations still confer a certain degree of respec-tability on their members. But that is not the way reputations are maintained any more. Were Max Weber to travel to North Carolina today, he would probably comment on the ease with which individuals qualify for credit by virtue of nothing more than a card with their name on it. A MasterCard or Visa is a modern day version of a club pin in the lapel.

Any but the very smallest intimate society will have some form of credential to establish trust. And the more mobile the population, the more dissociated such credentials will be from a particular locale. Sect membership in rural areas could not function as a credential when people moved frequently from rural to urban areas where such sects were not found or not known. In their place arose secular associations of a more national scope—the Masons, for example. Today, credentials are almost completely divorced from a particular location. And that is why they work so well as carriers of individual reputation.

Credit Cards

The use of credit predates the use of capital. Indentured servitude or loans with specific terms of repayment have been subject to regulation for well over a thousand years. The Code of Hammurabi (1750 B.C.) and the Old Testament of the Bible describe conditions under which credit may be extended and place restrictions on the creditors ability to extract a profit. Usury limitations or prohibitions are found in numerous legal and/or religious doctrines from that time to the present.

In the early days of the United States, virtually every state placed limits on the interest rates that could be charged by creditors (apparently for good reason, because the use of credit was quite common). "In fact, there is little, if any difference between the way credit is used in the United States today and the way it was used in the early 1800s, with the single exception of technology" (Mandell,1990:14). Farmers would promise re-payment after their harvest for implements, home furnishings, and other durables. Promissory notes were a conspicuous feature of rural econo-mies. City residents would often rely on installment credit arrangements for household durables—much as they do today. Credit terms resembled those of today. A down payment and a lien held by the merchant permitted urbanites to purchase a specific piece of furniture or other large household item and pay for it in installments. And finally there were frequent uses of "open book" credit accounts—found among retailers of inexpensive products such as foodstuffs and clothing. Consumers would sign for a purchase and settle with the merchant at the end of the month.

As historian Lewis Mandell notes, installment credit gained increasing popularity over the course of the nineteenth century. Industrialization produced relatively inexpensive large-ticket durables—sewing machines or stoves, for example. Consumers were allowed to purchase such items directly from salesmen who arranged the terms of the purchase. The Singer Sewing Machine Company was one of the first American firms to make widespread use of installment credit in the marketing of its popular product. By 1850 the practice was commonplace. By 1870 most all types of household appliances were available on credit.

The distinctive feature of all such arrangements was their two-party nature. A consumer and a vendor arranged the terms for the purchase of an item. There was no "third party" to the exchange. However, shortly after the Civil War third-party creditors became increasingly important. The small loan business made loans of cash to consumers to permit them to purchase items directly. Credit unions were legalized at the turn of the twentieth century thereby affording greater access to small loans from a third party source. And in 1910, Arthur J. Morris opened a bank in Chicago that made small loans to consumers at 6 percent annual interest rates. "Morris plan" banks spread to 37 states by 1920 (Mandell, 1990:15).

The rapid growth and use of third-party creditors following the Civil War occurred simultaneously with urbanization and industrialization of the country. Undoubtedly, industrialization had much to do with the spread of such financial arrangements—especially the need for significant loans to finance manufacturing. However, there is an equally important social factor that partially explains this development. Urbanization and migration disrupted hitherto intact communities of families. An industrial economy depends on easy migration of labor. In new and unfamiliar urban regions, migrants were isolated from their families and other familiar sources of financial assistance. At the same time, the standards of consumerism fostered greater needs for money. In cities, reputation depended as much on conspicuous symbols of status as it had on family name in an earlier and more rural time.

Writing at the turn of the century, political economist Thorstein Veblen noted that the basis of reputation changed with the development of industry. In particular he argued that symbols of worth became increasingly significant.

The possession of goods, whether acquired aggressively by one's own exertion or passively by transmission through inheritance from others, becomes a conventional basis of reputability. . . . Wealth confers honor on its possessor. . . . In any community where goods are held in severalty it is necessary, in order to his own peace of mind that an individual should possess as large a portion of goods as others with whom he is accustomed to class himself. (Veblen, 1961:561)

In sum, two forces operated to stimulate the growth and use of third-party creditors at the turn of the twentieth century: migration of "strangers" to cities and the entire set of economic and social conditions promoting pressures to consume. By the middle of the twentieth century, automobiles and electric appliances were being consumed increasingly and fueled dramatic growth in the use of consumer credit from third parties: finance companies, credit unions, and banks.

The growth of retail operations and the increasing density of cities made it more and more difficult for vendors to know who they were dealing with. Where open-book charge accounts were once routinely offered to familiar customers, the practice became more and more difficult in dense urban settings. A "stranger" who was qualified to receive credit at a department store needed something to establish his reputation as credit worthy. *A credit credential was needed.* That is how the problem was then viewed. The answer to this problem was the first credit card—a portable symbol of reputability that allowed an individual to trade on his good name despite the fact that the other party to the transaction had no idea who he was.

The credit card was not a novel form of financing. Since a large amount of retail trade already depended on credit, "the conversion of the retail charge account into a credit card was no more than a change in terminology" (Mandell, 1990:17). Department stores, restaurants, and oil companies were the first to distribute cards to their regular customers in the 1920s and 1930s.

Since its inception, the credit card has served as a convenient credential. Of course, that is not its primary purpose. Rather, credit cards were offered to consumers in hopes of stimulating consumerism and rationalizing bookkeeping. A metal charge plate, when inserted into an imprinting device, would record the sale, the name of the purchaser, and the relevant credit information. *The economic benefits of credit cards, however, have always been tempered by their reputational significance.* For example, Standard Oil Company of Indiana quickly distributed a quarter million new cards in 1939 to virtually any individual who owned an automobile. As the company soon learned, however, mass distribution of unsolicited credit cards generated more fraud and loss than it generated profit. Credit cards, we have learned, work when the individual holding them is certified (i.e., selected) as trustworthy. Undoubtedly, credit cards are a stimulus to purchasing. However, they cannot function unless they also guarantee the reputation of the user, unless, that is, they are also credentials of trustworthiness.

Those same forces that prompted the early development of credit cards were in even fuller force following World War II. The postwar economy was primed to afford a hitherto unknown level of consumerism as a result of higher wages and full employment. As Mandell (1990:22) notes, "Discretionary income, a term previously unknown to most Americans, became the watchword of this new era of growth in consumer credit." Rapid urbanization and migration also figured prominently in the reasons for the unparalleled growth of credit following the war. Growing populations of strangers were increasingly being offered a credential that permitted access to charge accounts.

The 1950s saw the full development of "revolving" credit—a system in which the consumer was given a fixed line of credit and required to pay one-sixth of the balance plus an interest charge of 1 percent on the unpaid balance each month. Though similar arrangements had existed on a small scale in the 1930s, it was Gimbel Bros. of New York who offered it on a widespread basis in 1947. Revolving credit was a solution to the desire to offer credit to less affluent customers who would not qualify for a regular charge account. The consumer with an income lower than required to establish a standard charge account might still qualify for a limited line of credit that required only partial repayment each month. This innovation made credit available to a vastly larger population.

In 1948, several large department stores in New York formed a cooperative credit card operation. Gimbel's, Saks, Bloomingdale's, Franklin Simon, and other similar retailers offered customers *one* card that could be used at a number of stores. Cards were notched to fit imprinting devices at those stores at which a customer had an account. Most importantly, this card was serviced by a central agency that distributed the cards, mailed bills, and maintained addresses. It was a first step toward the development of a centralized credit bureau that could certify an individual as credit worthy at more than one store. This seemingly simple arrangement set the stage for the development of the most significant advance in credit card use—the universal credit card.

The success of the department store cooperative credit plan led to similar, though vastly larger enterprises. There soon followed a number of "universal" credit card plans—credit cards that were issued by third parties and that could be used at a large number of establishments. Diners Club, formed in 1948, offered credit access to restaurants and hotels. The

American Express credit card was established in 1958 and within a year 32,000 establishments accepted the card, held then by almost half a million cardholders. Commercial banks also established universal credit cards. By the end of the 1950s, several large national banks, most notably Bank of America and Chase Manhattan Bank, were issuing revolving credit cards. Still, credit cards were issued by local banks and administered by them.

In the middle 1960s, several firms began to license their credit cards nationally. In 1966 Bank of America began to license its BankAmericard (later named Visa) and several other large banks formed a second national card system—the Interbank Card Association (later named Master Charge). Both BankAmericard and Interbank allowed a consumer to make a credit card purchase from a retailer anywhere in the United States. The national universal credit card was widely accepted and used by 1970.

One persistent obstacle for all major credit card operations was the establishment of a large cardholder base. Unsolicited mailings of cards, a strategy tried several times, were found unsatisfactory because of fraud and poor credit risks. In their search for a reliable method of establishing good risks, the dominant credit card operations began to rely on other credentials—especially educational degrees. In 1970, both Master Charge and BankAmericard offered free cards to almost any college student. While this strategy did not result in significant profits, it did indicate the growing importance of educational credentials for the establishment of economic trustworthiness.

As credit cards became more and more acceptable as a way of purchasing goods and services, they also assumed greater and greater significance as indicators of trustworthiness. Those who held credit were generally seen as more trustworthy than those who did not. The possession of a credit card might permit an individual to cash a check that, otherwise, might not be accepted. The credit card could be presented to a cashier as a form of "identification" permitting one to offer a check for the purchase of items.

The growing significance of credit, beyond its *purely* fiduciary implications, is dramatically shown by noting the rapid and increasing involvement of state and national legislatures in regulating the industry. Most credit card plans operate on rather low profit margins. Qualifying individuals for credit, therefore, must necessarily be a low-cost venture. Card companies initially relied almost exclusively on information provided on the application. The institution would apply various weights to each factor on the application to obtain a "credit score" (Mandell, 1990:56). And although this method may have satisfied the needs of banks and other financial institutions to distinguish between good and bad credit risks, it was opposed by civil rights groups as discriminatory since it relied on such characteristics as sex, age, marital status, and race. Two individuals alike on all other factors might fare quite differently in their applications for credit depending on their race or area of residence.

So important were credit cards and the credit they afforded that Congress was eventually forced to deal with the means used to qualify individuals for them. The first Equal Credit Opportunity Act was enacted by Congress in 1975. The bill prohibited the use of information on sex, race, and marital status in evaluating an application for a credit card. It required lenders to explain, in writing, why credit applications were denied. Women were granted their own credit records independent of their former husbands'.

The dramatic increase in demand for credit led, inevitably, to huge credit bureaus that maintained background information on vast numbers of individuals. Such computerized, centralized, and easily accessible information was essential for issuers of credit. By 1970 several national credit bureaus maintained information on significant numbers of people. Consumer activist Ralph Nader argued that two firms, Retail Credit Company and Capital Credit Data Corporation, maintained records on 72 million Americans in 1970. He argued that in addition to the legitimate use of such information by credit card firms, many others found this information tantalizing as well. Employers purchased credit reports on potential hires, and direct marketing firms purchased lists from credit bureaus to help target specific types of consumers. And the government, Nader alleged, used such information when conducting investigations of individuals (Mandell, 1990:59). In effect, credit bureaus are in the business of selling reputations. For a small fee, a credit record may be obtained for almost any individual who has been gainfully employed or who has applied for a loan.

Congress has been involved in numerous attempts to safeguard individuals' privacy by restricting access to individual credit records. The 1974 Federal Privacy Act and the Financial Institutions Regulatory and Interest Rate Control Act of 1978 placed minimal restrictions on such access. Still, however, it is very simple to purchase individual credit information for "legitimate purposes."

Today, because of large computerized systems, credit records are quickly and easily available as are authorizations for the use of credit cards. When presented with a credit card at the point of sale, a merchant is able to have the purchase authorized within a matter of seconds by tying into one of several national consumer credit processing centers. Clearly, the credit card is a highly portable credential. It establishes an individual's claim to financial trust and reputability.

Before proceeding, it is worth repeating that credit cards were invented for the purpose of identifying credit-worthy people who were not otherwise known to merchants. They were created to replace the reputation that allowed individuals in smaller communities simply to sign their names for a product.

The dramatic growth of credit card use since the late 1960s reflects many changes in the economy of the nation—especially the growing acceptance of installment buying. There has also been sustained effort to attract card holders, and there have been significant technological improvements made in the means of qualifying and authorizing sales on credit. As of 1989, barely more than 50 years after the birth of the credit card, approximately 62 percent of adults (110 million) had at least one credit card (Mediamark Research Inc., 1990:236).

In the effort to expand their cardholder base, credit card firms have recently begun to exploit the reputational significance of their cards. Most credit firms now offer, for a fee, cards that are intended to convey an impression although they offer only little in additional services or credit. Such "prestige" cards are predicted to be a major source of growth in credit cards in the next decade. "Gold Cards," for example, are ordinary credit cards—offering somewhat higher credit limits and additional services, and costing more—embossed in flashy gold plastic with conspicuous symbols intended to announce to all who see them that the holder is affluent, an exceptionally good credit risk, or is privileged among employees to special benefits. Additional benefits or credit lines do not explain the dramatic increase in the popularity of such "prestige" cards. None of the "prestige" cards looks like the ordinary version of the company's credit card. Each is designed to display conspicuously its distinctive reputational significance.

Research has shown that income and educational attainment are major predictors of who owns and uses credit cards. In 1989, for example, 82 percent of those whose incomes were above $60,000 held at least one credit card compared to only 54 percent of those whose family incomes were between $15,000 and $25,000. Those with even lower incomes have much lower rates of card holding. Similarly, while 83 percent of college graduates hold credit cards, only 40 percent of those with less than high-school education do (Mediamark Research, 1989:236; Canner, 1987). Age is also related to the use of credit; individuals in the prime work years (25 to 64) are most likely to own credit cards, while those younger or older are less likely to have cards.

Credit cards issued by banks (Visa or Mastercard) are more versatile and portable than store cards (J.C. Penny) , gasoline company cards, or travel cards. Research has shown that bank cards are more popular among individuals who travel or move frequently—those who do not have a visible and well-known local reputation among vendors. Indeed, one of the attractive features of major bank cards is their complete independence from local merchants or financial institutions. Bank credit cards are truly national or international. Furthermore, bank cards afford retailers access to an individual's credit worthiness *wherever* they are used. As such, a bank card is definitely a better credential than a local store card or other form of limited credit.

In their research of over 4,000 shoppers in two metropolitan regions, Hirschman, Alpert, and Strivastava (1989) found that store card users, as a group, were much more likely to be long-time residents of the area in which they were shopping. Bank card users, by contrast, were much more likely to be visitors or to have moved recently. For them, the bank card served as a very portable and effective credential.

If credit cards do, in fact, serve as credentials, it should be the case that their possession and use would increase as the number of individuals who need transportable, purchasable reputations increases. That is, individuals such as the emancipated would find credit cards (especially bank cards) particularly useful.

Data on the ownership of credit cards are surprisingly sparse. No federal governmental agency assembles reliable yearly figures. Nor does any other organization. The data used in the following figures were collected by two organizations. First, the Federal Reserve Board of the U.S. Government has commissioned several national surveys of consumer finances since 1970. These surveys are conducted by the Survey Research Center at the University of Michigan. The figure uses data taken from the 1970 Survey of Consumer Finances, the 1977 Consumer Credit Survey, the 1983 Survey of Consumer Finances, the 1984 Survey of Currency and Transaction Account Usage, the 1986 Survey of Consumer Attitudes, and the 1986 Survey of Consumer Finances.

To augment these data, marketing information assembled by Mediamark Research, Inc. of New York City is used. These data are compiled for the purposes of marketing and are drawn from probability samples of approximately 12,500 respondents yearly.

Figure 2 presents the percentage of emancipated young (age 20–24) males and females and the percentage of young persons (under age 25) who hold bank credit cards. These figures are crude, but are the best available at this time.

As Figure 2 demonstrates, the percentage of young adults who have bank credit cards has increased as the percentage of young adults who are emancipated has increased. Of course the overall rate of card ownership has increased dramatically since 1970. Much of that increase must be attributed to the aggressive marketing of the cards. However, the percentage of the U.S. population living alone has also increased, not just among

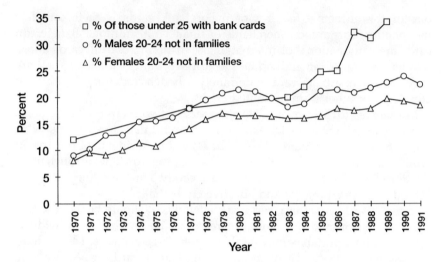

Figure 2. Trends in credit card ownership and emancipation: 1970–1989.

Source: For 1970–1983, figures are taken from Glenn B. Canner, 1987. "Changes in Consumer Holding and Use of Credit Cards, 1970–1986." *Journal of Retail Banking,* 18:13–24. For
1984–1989, figures are from Mediamark Research, Inc., 1990. *Banking, Investments, and Credit
Cards Report: Spring 1989,* Series P-6 and earlier volumes of this report.
   See Appendices A and B for figures used in all graphs.

the emancipated. Only 6 percent of Americans 16 and over lived alone in
1960. By 1990, slightly over 12 percent lived alone—a doubling in 30
years.

   The relationship between rates of youthful emancipation and the holding of bank credit cards by youths is consistent with the basic point I am
making in this chapter. Those who are unable to rely on more conventional methods of establishing a reputation (by reference to a family name or
long history of financial relationships) are more likely to rely on transportable reputations—credentials such as credit cards.

Drivers' Licenses

   Historian Joseph Kett, when describing the changing life course of
youths in America, states that since 1945, "acquisition of a driver's license
has become the rite of passage for middle-class American young people"
(Kett, 1977:265). Indeed, for most young Americans, acquiring a driver's
license is the most significant symbol of imminent adult rights and
responsibilities—of pending emancipation. Once licensed to drive, young

people have considerably greater freedoms and independence. In particular, driving permits significant escape from parental supervision. This, more than any other symbolic aspect of a driver's license makes it critical in defining the life course of young people.

In his discussion of the historic changes in the life course of youths in America, historian John Modell (1989:12, emphasis in original) notes: "Driving was not simply a privilege with obvious utility but also definitive of *a stage in one's life,* although admittedly one without a particular name attached to it." Moreover, it is adults who control the agencies that license drivers. Thus, changes in the age at which one may be licensed to drive may be viewed, in part, as reflecting popular sentiment about adolescence and young adulthood.

The national Uniform Drivers Code in 1926 established 16 as the minimum age for obtaining an unrestricted driver's license, and 14 for a learner's permit. Age provisions were not amended until 1962, when the lower limit for learner's permits was raised to 15 years. In 1968, however, there was a major revision in the code and the minimum age for unrestricted drivers' licenses was changed to 18 years. Most states now have 17 or 18 as the minimum age for obtaining a driver's license. This change was accompanied by a provision in most states that permitted younger people (16 or 17 depending on the state) to obtain licenses provided they had completed a certified driver's education course, or its equivalent. Additional restrictions have been applied to younger drivers—restricting the driver to daytime driving only, or requiring that the driver be accompanied by a licensed driver over the age of 18, for example [U.S. National Highway Traffic Safety Administration, 1980, Section 6–103 (a)].

Every state and territory of the United States now requires that motor vehicle drivers have a valid license to operate a motor vehicle. The first statewide drivers' license laws were enacted in 1903 in Massachusetts and Missouri; by 1954 all states required their drivers to be licensed. In addition, every state requires that motor vehicle drivers pass a written or oral test, a vision test, and a road test before a license can be issued. The first state to require an examination before issuing a license was Rhode Island, which enacted a law in 1908 requiring both a driver's license and an examination. (U.S. Department of Transportation, 1977:61)

The motivation for requiring drivers' licenses varied among regions and there is no comprehensive history of the establishment of automobile drivers' licenses. The experience of Chicago is illustrative, however. Soon after the turn of the century, motor vehicles began to compete with more conventional vehicles for the roadway. The most obvious characteristic of the automobile was, of course, its speed. Traveling at least twice the speed of horse-drawn carriages or trolleys, the automobile disrupted the orderly (homogeneous) flow of traffic on roads. "At 20 mph the motorcar could come to a stop in the same distance as a horse-drawn vehicle traveling at 10 mph, yet Chicago, like most other cities, confined the new machines to 8 mph—just below the average speed of a streetcar in traffic. The result was a great deal of lawbreaking, especially on boulevards and suburban roads, by citizens whose contact with officers of the law was otherwise very limited. . . . To be dealt with, the speeder had somehow to be *identified* and apprehended. Beginning in 1900, Chicago attempted to license all drivers by testing them in the mechanical and operational aspects of their vehicles" (Barrett, 1983:60, emphasis added). A series of 18 questions relating to the mechanism of the type of car to be driven, the responsibilities involved in operating a motor vehicle on city streets, and the applicant's past driving record were required of all automobile operators in Chicago (Flink, 1970:174). Public sentiment was clearly behind the idea of mandatory universal licensing. The November 1902 issue of *Horseless Age* reported, "The general sentiment of the leading automobile organizations and the public press seems to be favorable to it. A license law will prevent novices from driving to the common danger on public streets before they have acquired the requisite skill in manipulation of their vehicles, and perhaps, still more important, *will place automobile drivers under greater responsibility*" (in Flink, 1970:175, emphasis added).

The license, as these examples suggest, was a form of *identification* as much as it was a certification that the operator knew anything about how to operate the vehicle. But the idea of universal licensing did not catch on immediately. Despite widespread endorsement of the concept, only 12 states and the District of Columbia required all automobile drivers to obtain licenses in 1909. Another seven required licenses for all chauffeurs. Most interestingly, "The application forms for operators' licenses in these nineteen states as a rule asked for little more information than the applicant's name, address, age, and the type of automobile he claimed to be competent to drive" (Flink, 1970:178). In short, the earliest drivers' licenses were little more than formal identification cards. If anything, the identification function of a driver's license has increased over the years.

A reputation is a collection of impressions and evaluations. As I have noted, our actions toward others are guided, in part, by their reputations as well as a concern over our own. In a society of strangers, identification is clearly problematic. No matter what the form of credential, its reputational value depends on proper identification of its holder. The customer who wishes to use the credit afforded her by a credit card must first establish that she is, in fact, who she claims to be. The driver's license is, therefore, both credential (entitlement to certain privileges) and identification. That its identification function has become ever more important is understandable in light of the dramatic growth of strangers in our society. By what other means may strangers establish that they are, in fact, who they claim to be?

If there is such a thing as a national identification card, the drivers' license is it. Embossed with a photograph, a current address, a validated signature, and (often) a Social Security number, the license is routinely requested by merchants when asked to accept a check, by vendors of alcohol to validate a young person's age, by voter registrars to enfranchise individuals, or by numerous others who need some reliable form of personal identification. So important is the driver's license as a form of identification that since 1979 all states provide, for a fee, a personal identification card that resembles a drivers license in all aspects except that it clearly states that it is not a driver's license (U.S. Department of Transportation, 1982:79). A driver's license is the only form of identification held by a majority of Americans and controlled and distributed by the State. In 1989, 79 percent of females and 91 percent of males (aged 16 and older) in America held driver's licenses. In all, 165 million Americans hold licenses (as of 1989). The overall percentage of driving-age individuals licensed to drive has increased from 57 percent in 1950 to 86 percent in 1989 The number holding identification cards issued by Departments of Motor Vehicles is not known (U.S. Department of Transportation, 1991).

Because so much law governs driving, it is small wonder the license is almost universally regarded as a reliable form of identification. The Uniform Vehicle Code (a compilation of statutes from the various states and a source of uniformity in state driver license laws) states:

(a) Every application for an instruction permit or for a driver's license shall be made upon a form furnished by the department. Every application shall be accompanied by a birth certificate or other proof of the applicant's date of birth that is satisfactory to the department. (b) Every said application shall state the full name, date and place of birth, sex, and residence address of the applicant, and briefly describe the applicant (section 6–106). (U.S. Department of Transportation, 1980:106)

As proof of who one is, as an identification or certificate of identity, the driver's license is unparalled. Before issuing a license, the State examines applicants' abilities and fitness in very general terms. To receive a driver's license, one must prove he or she is of legal age, must be certified to have good eyesight, be able to read or otherwise understand written instructions, to have sufficient physical dexterity to actually operate a motor vehicle, and to be free of serious physical and mental disabilities—in short, to have minimal physical and intellectual skills (Section 6–110).

And once issued, the license contains valuable information about a person: an identification number (in a minority of states the Social Security Number), the full name, date of birth, residence address, a brief description, a color photograph, and one's usual signature (Section 6–111).

One indication of how important a license is for purposes of identification is the growing problem of counterfeiting. In the past 10 years, almost every state (43 in 1989) redesigned its license to make it more difficult to alter or counterfeit. In some states, the card is issued in plastic while in others the license is embossed with tamper-proof features. In the near future, holographic insignias are to be added to the license thereby making it impossible to reproduce.

Every state requires that driver's licenses be renewed at intervals ranging from 2 to 4 years (since 1938) (note: Alaskan licenses are renewed every 5 years). While renewals do not typically require all that much examination, without exception, applicants must complete a new application form and attest to its correctness by signing it. In most states, applicants must also submit to a visual exam.

The driver's license is keyed to a file of information maintained by the state on every individual who holds, has held, or has applied for a license. Such records indicate whether a license has been revoked for any reason (habitual traffic offenses, driving under the influence), a complete record of any traffic accidents, and abstracts of court records of convictions known to the State. This entire record is available (in almost every state) to *any* person who requests it and pays a nominal fee. The Uniform Vehicle Code (Section 6–117) states:

> (c) The department shall upon request furnish any person a certified abstract of the operating record of any driver. Such an abstract shall include enumeration of any accidents in which the driver has been involved, convictions, and information pertaining to financial responsibility.

Driving records are routinely requested by insurance carriers, potential employers, and prosecutors.

Even so good a system of identification suffers from very serious problems of accuracy. In particular, migration from one state to another requires that individuals obtain, from the state to which they moved, a new license. Each state requires new residents to surrender any valid license held from another state prior to receiving a new permit. That such a system does not work is reflected in the fact that there are more drivers' licenses than persons of driving age in some populous states (U.S. Department of Transportation, Driver's Licensing Laws Annotated, 1980:106). Part of the problem is administrative—it is not yet possible to determine whether an applicant for a driver's permit is licensed in another state. Part of the problem is due to fraud—some persons obtain driver's licenses in several states for the purpose of avoiding the consequences of traffic violations.

The National Driver Registrar (NDR) is a computer master file that consists of an abstract from State driver records for each person whose license to operate motor vehicles has been revoked, suspended, or denied. The NDR exists to aid State licensing programs in identifying problem drivers. It presently contains 22 million records on about 12 million individuals. This information is available not only to driver licensing officials, but also to federal agencies charged with investigating accidents (e.g., National Transportation Safety Board) (U.S. Department of Transportation, Driver' Licensing Laws Annotated, 1980:9).

Data on drivers licenses are maintained by the U.S. Department of Transportation and are published annually in a report titled "Highway Statistics." The figures used for the following graph were taken from annual reports from 1963 (the first available year) to 1989. For each year, the number of licenses in effect for individuals aged 20 to 24 was recorded and divided by the U.S. Census Bureau estimate of the number of individuals of that age. The result was expressed as a percentage and may be interpreted as an estimate of the percentage of youths (20 to 24) who hold drivers licenses. It must be remembered that the numerator of this percentage is likely to be an overestimate because of the problems of duplicate licenses. However, given the relatively young age of the population of interest, duplicate permits are not all that common.

Against these estimates are plotted the percentage of youths (20 to 24) who are emancipated. The results for males and females are presented together in Figure 3.

It is immediately apparent that male and female trends differ significantly. For males, virtually all were estimated to be licensed to drive in 1963 (96 percent) whereas only 69 percent of females that year held driver's licenses. The percentage of licensed young men dropped by about 4 percent in 1968–1969 with the introduction of higher minimum ages for obtaining permits. No comparable drop was recorded among females at that time. Since 1968, the percentage of young men holding drivers permits has been almost constant. It reached a peak between 1975 and 1977 (95 and 96 percent) but hovered around 92 to 93 percent for the rest of the 1970s and 1980s.

The relationship between emancipation and possession of drivers' licenses among *males* is not what would be predicted by the argument I am making. There was no increase in licensure that corresponded with the increase so obvious in emancipation. Indeed, the correlation between emancipation and driver's license rates for males is actually negative, r =

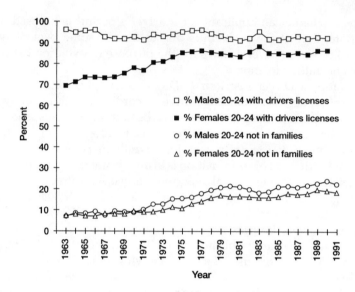

Figure 3. Trends in drivers licenses and emancipation: 1963–1990.

Source: U.S. Department of Transportation, Federal Highway Administration. 1963. *Highway Statistics,* and annual volumes of this report since 1963.

See Appendices A and B for figures used in all graphs.

–.35. In contrast, the relationship for females is quite strong and clear; the correlation of .85 summarizes a very strong association. Why might emancipation correlate with driver's permits for females but not for males?

One of the most obvious explanations focuses on the data. Since the series began in 1963 when 96 percent of young males were licensed to drive, there was no way that the rates could go up—they were already close to their maximum. If virtually every young man held a driver's license in 1968, it would not matter that emancipation rates tripled between then and 1989 since there could not be a notable increase over the level established in the late 1960s. Perhaps data from the 1950s onward might more closely track emancipation rates. We cannot know if this is so because we do not have the necessary data. In short, drivers' licenses may operate as other credentials do for males, but they are almost universally held and have been since at least 1963.

Alternatively, drivers' licenses may, indeed, operate as credentials for boys—but may do so in a somewhat different way. The interpretation I offer focuses on the elaboration of adolescence and premarital courtship in the post-World War II era. Drivers' licenses became central to adolescent identity among boys born in the Baby Boom, a consequence of the development of the novel custom of "dating." Viewed this way, the acquisition of a driver's permit was as central a form of credential among *unemancipated* boys as the educational degree or a credit history was among the emancipated.

The automobile figures prominently in the rise of dating and the methods by which dates were conducted. Writing in 1938, sociologist Willard Waller described the competitive aspect of dating, calling it the "rating and dating complex" (Waller, 1938:234). Waller noted how individuals tended to date others of comparable "worth" as judged by their peers. "The tendency is for Class A men to date principally Class A women. Young men are desirable dates according to their rating on the scale of campus values. In order to have Class A rating they must belong to one of the better fraternities, be prominent in activities, have a copious supply of spending money, be well-dressed. . . *and have access to an automobile*" (Waller, 1938:232,emphasis added).

Rating and dating were conspicuous aspects of high school culture as early as the 1940s. As historian Beth Bailey notes in her aptly titled book *From Front Porch to Back Seat* (1988:30–31)

> Rating, dating, popularity, competition: catchwords hammered home, reinforced from all sides until they seemed a natural vocabulary. You had to rate in order to date, to date in order to rate. To stay popular you competed. There was no end. . . you competed to become popular, and being popular allowed you to continue to compete. *Competition* was the key term in the formula—remove it and there was no rating, dating, or popularity.

By the mid-1950s, frequent dates with many others had largely given way to the custom that came to be called "going steady" popularly viewed as an imitation of early marriage. Going steady removed some of the competitive aspects of dating. But not all. Still, women were portrayed as commodities that a successful male could acquire. An automobile was a central component in the male ego. "The equation of women and cars was common in mid-century American culture. Both were property and both were expensive; cars and women came in different styles or models, and both could be judged on performance. The woman he escorted, just as the car he drove, publicly defined both a man's taste and his means" (Bailey, 1988:70).

As going steady gained in popularity, so did greater sexual permissiveness. Throughout the 1960s, sexual norms governing dating became more and more lenient. But no matter how permissive might be youth culture, privacy was required to enjoy the freedoms. Cars were generally viewed as the best and most private option for sexual privacy. So great was the concern over unsupervised sexual privacy that local governments often sought to regulate the use of automobiles for sex—forbidding individuals to remain in parked automobiles without the lights being on, for example, or forbidding parking in certain popular areas (Bailey, 1988:87).

The traditional date of the 1960s and early 1970s had a well-known script. The young man called several days ahead to invite the young woman out. He would suggest a time and place for the evening. On the night of the date, he would drive to her house or apartment in his own or his family's car. He would take her out, and pay for everything. Later, the young man would drive to some secluded spot, park the car, and the couple would "park"—neck, pet, or "make out." The car was crucial to the entire event.

If one views access to the automobile as a central component of youthful dating, it becomes easier to understand why almost all young men held drivers' licenses by the mid-1960s. Dating then, as is well documented, was largely "run" by men. Males arranged dates, decided where to go, and paid for the evening. In return, some degree of sexual intimacy was expected. The car gave young men (and young women) freedom from parental supervision. But access to an automobile was not nearly so central to a young woman's self-concept because men provided the resources for a date. Without a car, a young man in the 1960s and early 1970s was severely limited in what he could offer a girl for a date. A young girl suffered nothing for lack of a car.

The formality of dating and going steady gradually lost popularity. As casual mixed-sex groupings and "hanging out" have come to replace structured weekend-night dates, males and females have accepted greater and greater equality. Access to an automobile is simply less crucial for "success" in the male–female affairs of young people today. In today's world, a young male is able to be popular with young women without an automobile—at least more so than was his father 30 years ago.

Drivers' licenses, therefore, have served as an essential credential in the youthful male life course. Without one, a young man had limited opportunities for dating. Without one, his popularity was assuredly jeopardized. Driving was a central element in the young man's appeal. Driving was, essentially, a form of emancipation in itself. It afforded an escape from the watchful eyes of parents and others. It permitted some degree of privacy. To the extent that youthful courtship has abandoned the structured date as an essential component of masculinity (or femininity), access to the automobile is somewhat less crucial.

Whether the slight declines in young males' rates of holding drivers licenses can be traced to the declining significance of the automobile in dating cannot be known. Surely, young people today have greater access, overall, to automobiles than has any prior generation. My point is that such access may be important for many reasons. But it is less and less central to the sexual ego of the young man—at least as it depends on popularity with females.

Educational Degrees

The history of education in America makes it quite clear that schooling has served many purposes. Quite aside from the utilitarian goals of producing competence in certain skills, education is a dominant form of social control. Through schools, our society has structured the life course of young people in accordance with prevailing beliefs about human development and concerns over morality. Schools are powerful organizations that affect virtually every member of our society. By considering how the structure of education has changed over time, we are able to see the growing importance of educational degrees as credentials in a society of strangers.

As noted earlier, historian Joseph Kett described how a new view of childhood emerged in the mid-nineteenth century. Between 1840 and 1880 a view came to be accepted that the "internalization of moral restraints and the formation of character were more likely to succeed in planned, engineered environments than in casual ones" (Kett, 1977:112). Where adult supervision and monitoring had once been the primary mechanism for controlling young people's experiences, internal controls began to supplement this. Guilt, not shame, could produce conformity among youths. This change in thinking ushered in a greater emphasis on structuring and regimenting the experiences of young people. Youth, in short, was coming to be seen for the first time as formative. Schools were seen as important players in the essential task of fostering internalized moral standards.

Changing beliefs are reflected in the growing significance of *age*. If youthful experiences are believed to contribute to the sort of adult one becomes—that the personality develops cumulatively—then age assumes great significance. The very young child must be segregated from older youths lest his or her development suffer.

Kett observes how Sunday schools became more and more age homogeneous in the mid-nineteenth century. Where Sunday schools had once been philanthropic attempts to influence the children of the poor, middle-class youths began regular attendance in age-segregated programs. The same thing occurred in secular education. Age grading became more and more commonplace and the school year lengthened from weeks to months. Schooling came to have tremendous significance in a world filled increasingly with migrants and strangers. The importance of *religious conversion* (previously of tremendous significance) was significantly less critical than the other factors associated with attending school.

> The child was, as ever, father to the man, but now in the sense that childhood formed a mold which determined later development, rather than in the traditional sense that the occurrences of childhood were indications of later direction and prospects. . . . The common school revival . . . gave public education a mighty push in the direction of environmental control. (Kett, 1977:116, 122)

The concern over regulating youthful experiences made high schools increasingly important. By the end of the nineteenth century, in fact, attendance was mandatory during the "dangerous" years of adolescence. Attendance at high schools meant that youths remained at home longer. Too early departure from home came to be seen as a problem and fewer young people, in fact, left home. Attendance at academies declined as did apprenticeship; young people were expected to live continuously under their parents' roof until they left home for good.

Sociologist Randall Collins argues that the growth of educational credentialism in twentieth century America can be traced, in large part, to massive and ethnically diverse immigration at the turn of the century (Collins, 1979) Public education, he argues, was used "both as a means of control and of monopolization by the Anglo-Protestant bourgeoisie, and eventually as a path to creating positions and to occupational mobility by many immigrant groups themselves" (Collins, 1979:79). Immigration of massive numbers of aliens produced cultural diversity of a level previously unknown. The new immigrants were viewed as strangers— individuals who lacked reputations and who could not be trusted.

Collins points out that unlike almost every other industrial society, American education is a *contest mobility* system. Most societies divide their secondary education among several institutions: an elite system (the English public school or the French lyceé) leading to university attendance, a commercial high school that prepares students for business or clerical work; and sometimes a third sector for engineers and technicians or vocational arts. Once a student has reached a crucial branching point, he or she is tracked into one of these. And once in the particular branch, the student is not expected continually to compete to remain in it. There is much less focus on testing and other forms of overt, conspicuous competition. Such a system has been called a *sponsored mobility* system (Turner, 1960) A contest mobility system such as ours lacks crucial branching points. There are no sharp divisions among secondary schools and it is easy to transfer among different sorts of programs or reenter after dropping out (Collins, 1979:91).

Until the middle nineteenth century, and the beginnings of massive waves of immigration however, schooling in America was not at all a contest system. Rather, education took place in many locations, notably apprenticeships, churches and private schools, and, in rare instances, private academies. Basic literacy and skills might be acquired at home or in school. As Collins notes, schooling was much less structured and formal. "Elementary schools and apprenticeship were for the artisan class; the Latin grammar schools and the colleges for the upper class; and academies emerged in the eighteenth century, with a somewhat less classical curriculum, for the urban commercial middle class" (Collins, 1979:104). These forms of education, however, were not articulated— entrance into one did not require prior certification from another. Indeed, certification was not a conspicuous feature of educational institutions. Even those few individuals who attended college typically received no actual degree or diploma.

The first half of the nineteenth century witnessed the creation of a public elementary school system in most states. And by 1880 a majority of those under age 18 were enrolled. Beginning around 1860, public high schools began to emerge and by the end of the century attendance at them was mandatory in a majority of U.S. states. The public high-school movement was strongest in the cities of the nation where immigrants were most conspicuous. And immigrants and their "alien" cultures were important in the development of public high schools.

Whereas three-quarters of the adult male population of the United States in 1850 was native born, this figure was only 55 percent 15 years later (U.S. Bureau of the Census, 1975: Series C 218–283). And whereas the overwhelming majority of foreign born residents in 1850 had immigrated from Protestant countries (northwestern Europe) by 1900 half were from northern Europe. "By 1890 the Catholics and Jews probably outnumbered the white Protestants in the United States" (Collins, 1979:97).

The ethnic diversity created by immigration was reflected in very obvious differences in values and beliefs as well as life-styles and habits of mind. Broad differences in social class background, work habits, and political ideologies were associated with the religious diversity found among immigrants. Anglo-Protestants tended to view the new arrivals with great suspicion if not outright enthnocentric prejudice. Protestant homogeneity was giving way to ethnic diversity and, as this happened, Protestant control of American culture eroded.

Rather predictably, conservative Protestants attempted to regain some of the cultural centrality they were losing. Religious revivals in the urban areas of America were an attempt to instill in the immigrants some of the dominant cultural traits of Anglo-Protestants. Other "reform" efforts in the cities, such as the settlement house movement, attempted much the same thing. All attempted to "Americanize" immigrants—to make them less like strangers.

But the most significant attempt to restore the dominant culture was through education. As Collins notes, public schools with compulsory attendance laws spread mainly in those states facing the greatest immigration influx; the claims of educators to Americanize the immigrants was a major force in getting public support (Collins, 1979:102). It is the ethnic diversity of late nineteenth and early twentieth century America that Collins believes accounts for our contest-mobility educational credential system. Education and degrees are mediums that allowed diverse populations to compete with a common "currency."

So what is it that schools actually "taught"? In general it is safe to say that a liberal arts curriculum has been the standard in American public schools since their inception. There has never been a truly significant vocational education alternative to regular high school even while parents and educators may have recognized the lack of practical utility of a liberal education. Training has always been available on the job. But public schools have offered social mobility via college. No corresponding advantage inheres to vocational training. And mobility is a cornerstone of American public schools. As such, educational credentials figure prominently in their overall missions.

As Kett (1977:153) observed: "A diploma could act as a kind of letter of introduction. What did a diploma certify? Certainly literacy, but also manners. . . the near obsession with deportment reflected a desire to socialize and Americanize immigrants and their children."

Once colleges began to require high school completion for entrance, and once graduate and professional schools required college completion for entrance (in the 1890s), educational credentials were essential for social mobility (Kett, 1977).

The demand for credentials to enter professions soon emerged. Numerous professions (law, medicine, dentistry, veterinary medicine, pharmacy) established professional credentials near the turn of the twentieth century.

The influx of immigrants played an important role in the restructuring of professions—that is, in the establishment of credentials. Immigrants threatened the elite image of certain professions like law—especially as immigrants were Jews or other non-Protestant groups. Just as education was used to Americanize alien strangers, educational credentials were viewed as a means to maintain existing standards—largely WASP control over the professions.

The burgeoning of certification requirements after 1880 which accompanied the proliferation of professional schools had less to do with the growing complexity of occupations than with the attitudes and ideals of promoters of professional education . . . College degrees were credentials by 1900. Those who obtained them were assured leadership positions in business on graduation. It was the "intangible" benefits of education being rewarded—a spirit of competition and ambition. (Kett, 1977:155, 172)

An educational degree was minimal assurance that an individual held certain beliefs and values. It offered some degree of confidence that such a person could be trusted to do certain things. It produced, in short, a reputation.

Over the years, the professions have repeatedly increased the entrance requirements by relying on higher and higher educational attainments. And, correspondingly, the educational industry has expanded dramatically over those years. The rise of credentialism in professions led to emulation by less respected occupations—especially business occupations such as accounting.

The entire argument outlined above locates the driving force behind educational credentialism in the professionals and other elites concerned over the erosion of their privileges and positions. However, viewed from a slightly different perspective, the process was driven by growing numbers of strangers. Whether or not immigrants were actually a threat to the status quo can never be known. But that they were perceived to be is quite clear. It was immigrants' strangeness, their different ways and beliefs that fostered demands for mandatory schooling and credentials. It was a lack of familiarity with them that drove the process.

No matter how strongly any group might have wished to have its position safeguarded by the establishment of social structures—schools or licensing boards, for example—it was surely impossible to implement such broad and sweeping changes unilaterally. A population had to be convinced that things like mandatory schooling made sense. There clearly was a time in our history when it did not as evidenced by the absence of such things. The crucial theoretical question is why, at a particular moment in history (the late nineteenth century in this case), these changes did make sense—why the concerns of educational elites, clergy, and professionals were met with growing acceptance. The argument I am making is that credentials and the schools that produced them were palatable because of the changing composition of the population—the density and diversity associated with population growth, urbanization, and immigration made conventional forms of reputations unknowable or unreliable as a basis for trust. In their place, portable, objective reputations were created: educational credentials.

The development of such portable reputations is also consistent with the changed world view that sees development as a cumulative process.

In the same historical era that educational credentials first became conspicuous there was a growing emphasis on the inculcation of self-restraint. Guilt was gradually coming to replace shame as a form of social control. Self-restraint could be accomplished, or so it was reasoned, in very structured educational environments.

If, in fact, educational credentials serve as portable reputations, then they should be in greater abundance as the number of strangers in a society increases. As the number of young people who do not live in families increases, there should be a corresponding increase in educational credentials. More specifically, if we were to witness an increase in emancipation among young people of a certain age, we should then witness an increase in their possession of educational credentials.

To determine whether or not this has happened, I have recorded for each year since 1947 the percentage of 20 to 24 year olds who do not live in families. I have also recorded the percentage of young adults (25 to 29) who hold at least a college degree (who have completed four years of college).

One might object that there would necessarily be a relationship between these two sets of figures because college attendance often requires emancipation—students often live in college dormitories. This, however, is not an issue in the trends plotted in Figure 4. The U.S. Census Bureau counts college students living away from home (in dormitories, for example) as residents of their *parents'* household so long as they are dependents. Thus, any increase in emancipation due to college residence away from home is not reflected in the emancipation series used here. This has two consequences. First, the estimate of emancipation I am using is an underestimate because over 2 million individuals live in dormitories (1990) (U.S. Bureau of the Census, 1991b: Table 74) Second, the relationship between emancipation rates and credential rates is not confounded by emancipation due to college attendance.

The single measure of educational credentials I will use here is the percentage of young adults (25 to 29) who have completed *at least* a college degree (estimated in some years by the percentage who have completed at least four years of college). Undoubtedly there are many other forms of educational credentials than a college diploma. However, high school completion, while not universal, approaches that. Other forms of educational credentials are so rare as to be less informative (GED for example).

Figure 4 reveals the very close association between rates of emancipation and college completion rates for both males and females. Very low levels of both emancipation and college completion rates are recorded for 1947. In that year, only 3 percent of males and females between the ages of

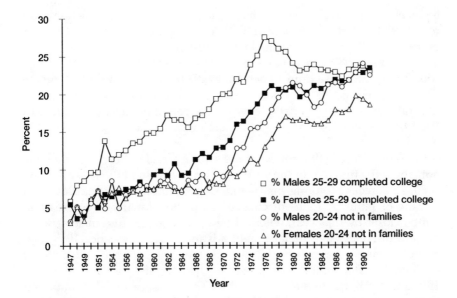

Figure 4. Trends in college completion and emancipation: 1947–1991.

Source: U.S. Bureau of the Census, Current Population Reports, Series P-20. Figures are from the *Educational Attainment* reports since 1947.

*Educational attainment figures were not reported for the years 1948, 1949,1951,1954,1955,1956,1958,1960, 1961, and 1963. The values used in the graph are estimates produced by a linear regression equation estimated for the years between 1947–1976 for which figures were available.

See Appendices A and B for figures used in all graphs.

20 and 24 did not live in families and only 5.8 and 5.4 percent of males and females 25 to 29 held college credentials.

By the height of the Baby Boom (1960) 7 percent of both males and females were living outside of families and college completion had risen notably among males (to 15 percent) and modestly among females (to 9 percent). Rates of emancipation continued their upward climb through the 1960s increasing modestly for both males and females. During that decade, college completion rates rose in tandem. Thus, by 1970, one-fifth of males 25 to 29 and slightly under one-eighth of females that age had earned college degrees while about one-tenth of both sexes (20 to 24) lived outside of families.

The 1970s was the decade of the greatest change in both emancipation and college completion. By 1980, 21 percent of young males and 16 percent of young females lived outside of families—an increase of 12 and

8 percent, respectively. During that same period college completion rates rose and fell largely in accord with emancipation rates. By 1976, 28 percent of college-age males had earned degrees but the rate declined to 24 percent by 1980. For females, a comparable change occurred. College completion rates rose from 13 percent in 1970 to 21 percent in 1977 where they remained in 1980. For both sexes, therefore, the increase in completion rates was most dramatic between the beginning and the middle of the 1970s, leveling off or declining somewhat in the second half of the decade.

Rates of emancipation followed the same general pattern—rising most notably in the first half of the 1970s and much less so in the latter half. By 1980, 22 percent of young males and 16 percent of young females lived outside of families. Rates of college completion for the two sexes had gotten closer by that year, when 24 percent of college-age males and 21 percent of college-age females held advanced degrees. Since 1980 only modest changes have occurred in either emancipation or educational credentials. After a notable drop in emancipation rates for males (between 1980 and 1983), the rate rebounded by 1990. Rates for females continued their steady increase through the 1980s. The drop in emancipation rates among males was matched by a drop in college completion rates at roughly the same time. Trends for females in the 1980s showed similar correspondence—both moving up or remaining stable in tandem.

The basic trends revealed in this graph lend strong support to the idea that emancipation and credentials (as measured here) are strongly correlated. Indeed, correlations between the two trends are both (male and female) quite strong, $r=.88$ for males and $r=.94$ for females. Equally strong correlations are found when high-school completion (rather than college completion) is used as the measure of credentials. Sophisticated time-series techniques that control for the year-to-year trends (serial correlation) and focus only on the simultaneous increases and decreases in the trends produce the same basic conclusion. In sum, there is very strong evidence here to link emancipated and educational credentials.

Conclusion

When people lose or misplace their purse or wallet, they typically react with great alarm. Although there may have been some amount of money lost, the greater problem is the loss of various cards and licenses. Without our wallets, we will surely have trouble cashing a check or conducting other forms of business. What we carry in our wallets is our public reputation, our proof of entitlement to various benefits and privileges. The person who has no such "identification" is an anomaly today.

But when did Americans begin to carry their reputations in their hip pockets and purses? And why? In this chapter I have attempted to show how the growing density and mobility of our population contributed to this practice. The twentieth century was the first in which average people needed portable proof of who they were, or of their credit worthiness. The "secularization" of America that Max Weber described at the turn of the century was the beginning of the process. Credit cards, drivers licenses, and educational credentials (among many others) are the badges we now wear in our buttonholes. These things permit anonymous strangers to conduct business as though they knew one another.

Credentials do not, however, say that much about a person. In fact, the information conveyed by credentials is actually rather minimal. But reputations are always sketchy images. We really do not need or care to know that much about other people. A simple distinction between those who do and who do not play by the same rules is all we really need. With more and more privacy, however, it is increasingly difficult to make such distinctions and there is every reason to believe that more stringent forms of surveillance will be an acceptable tradeoff in the future.

Surveillance in the form of credentials is one of the prices we willingly pay for vastly expanded amounts of privacy. So much of our lives now lie beyond the legitimate scrutiny of others, we proclaim ourselves trustworthy by presenting evidence that is objectively maintained by "third parties." Credit bureaus, Boards of Education and Accreditation, and the State are legitimate bureaucracies entrusted with our names. Collectively, we have established these social structures to replace regular and routine monitoring by our neighbors and friends.

A lie is, indeed, quite consequential in a society of strangers because so much depends on the faith we have in one another's truthfulness. Lacking the personal information necessary to discern the veracity of others' claims, we trust instead the monitoring provided by large social structures. Credit bureaus maintain "bad risk" files, and the National Driver Registrar maintains information on those who have had their license to drive suspended or rescinded. The records of college and university registrars are guarded more closely and governed by more state and federal law than virtually any other records in higher education. All such systems help us to recognize the truth or falsity of claims made by others.

Credentials alone, however, are increasingly inadequate for this purpose. As noted in this chapter, virtually any type of credential is potentially subject to fraud. As we become increasingly suspicious of credentials, we turn increasingly to alternative methods. If we believe that credentials are subject to perversion, we must augment them. And we do so, increasingly I argue, with ordeals. The presumption of distrust competes with the presumption of trust. When we begin an association with another person on that basis, we may afford that person an opportunity to dispute or disprove the presumption—an opportunity to establish their innocence or their claims. That is the purpose and definition of an ordeal—the topic of the next chapter.

4

ORDEALS

O creature of water, I adjure thee by the living God, by the holy God who in the beginning separated thee from the dry land; I adjure thee by the living God who led thee from the fountain of Paradise, and in four rivers commanded thee to encompass the world; I adjure thee by Him who in Cana of Galilee by His will changed thee to wine, who trod on thee with His holy feet, who gave thee the name Siloa; I adjure thee by the God who in thee cleansed Naaman, the Syrian, of his leprosy; saying, O holy water, O blessed water, water which washest the dust and sins of the world, I adjure thee by the living God that thou shalt show thyself pure, nor retain any false image, but shalt be exorcised water, to make manifest and reveal and bring to naught all falsehood, and to make manifest and bring to light all truth; so that he who shall place his hand in thee, if his cause be just and true, shall receive no hurt; but if he be perjured, let his hand be burned with fire, that all men may know the power of our Lord Jesus Christ, who will come, with the Holy Ghost, to judge with fire the quick and the dead, and the world! Amen!

Formulae Exorcismorum, in Lea (1973:34)

Introduction

Having said these words, a priest instructed one accused of a crime or one hoping to defend his innocence to plunge his hand into a caldron of boiling water and retrieve a ring or rock. Having done so, the hand was carefully wrapped in a cloth and sealed with the judge's mark. After 3 days, the hand was unwrapped and examined. If the hand was badly burned and blistered, the accused was judged guilty. If the hand was "clean," healing normally without signs of great injury, the party was judged innocent. About half of those undergoing such a trial were found to be guilty. This form of ordeal was the most widely used of the many medieval varieties of such methods for resolving disputes.

Such inhuman endeavors are almost incomprehensible to us today. It seems impossible that anyone could be put through such an ordeal in modern times. In fact, ordeals are used quite extensively today and substantially for the same reasons as in medieval Europe. And at least some of those subjected to modern day ordeals end up being victims of great injustice.

Far from being archaic methods of verifying "truth" that were abandoned in favor of more objective means, ordeals are today a conspicuous feature of modern society. Where ancients appealed to *God* to render a verdict when humans could not, modern ordeals appeal to *science* for a verdict. Both ancient and modern ordeals require a human to interpret the "evidence." As such, both are inherently subjective methods of verifying truth. But ordeals are never seen that way. Instead, the subjective human agent involved is not a conspicuous feature of the ordeal. Rather, it is the objective, unimpeachable verdict of God or science on which the ordeal focuses.

Ordeals are a form of surveillance. They establish or maintain reputations. As with credentials, the use of ordeals will be shown to be a function of the extensiveness of *strangers;* those who lack reputations. Since privacy is a major factor in the increase in strangers, ordeals are a consequence of privacy.

An ordeal is a ritual that determines whether an individual is telling the truth. It begins with a presumption of guilt or unresolvable doubt. A verdict is determined by an appeal to a nonhuman, sometimes supernatural, power. Often, the proof of innocence depends on the appearance of a "miracle"—a result that is not within the realm of ordinary reactions to events and one believed possible only if ordained by a supernatural agency: an unburned hand after plunging it into boiling water or carrying a red hot bar of iron, sinking when bound and thrown into water, causing a corpse to bleed by touching it, or surviving the ingestion of poison. The accused whose hand did not suffer tremendous damage by carrying a red hot bar of iron seven paces was viewed as having been acquitted or vindicated by the powers of God, to whom the problem was appealed and from whom a decision was expected. Ultimately, however, it was a *human* who interpreted these signs. The priest who rendered a decision on the results of the ordeal was required to *interpret* the evidence. But the verdict was not viewed as originating with the human. Instead, it was viewed as originating with God.

Ordeals are a way of validating a reputation, of supporting the claims made by one person against another, or of resolving the uncertainty associated with a contentious charge. The cause of an ordeal was, immediately, doubt (although ordeals may have also served as a form of torture). Only when an individual's word could not be trusted was that person subjected to the ordeal. The distinguishing feature of all ordeals was the involvement of a higher authority—a god or nonhuman power—to resolve mundane human doubts and disputes. Only when human agencies were unable to answer the question was it appealed to a higher authority. And once the ordeal was conducted and an answer given, there was no further appeal. Who, after all, could dispute the word of God? The ordeal was, therefore, the highest order of dispute resolution—the court of last resort.

A Brief History of Ordeals

Historians date the first recorded reference to the ordeal to around 510 A.D. in the first revision of the Salic law (among Germanic tribes). Later sixth century additions to the Salic Law and also the Ripurian law (Ripurians were a group of Franks who settled along the Rhine near Cologne in the fourth century) contain provisions for administering the ordeal of the cauldron. As such, the ordeal is generally regarded as a Frankish invention (see Bartlett, 1986). Bartlett showed that references to ordeals outside the Frankish world occurred only *after* the sixth century, the earliest of which is in Irish law. Ordeals were used at that time as a common method for resolving disputes over the rights and property of kindred. They were also prescribed in law to resolve disputes arising from theft, false witness, and contempt of court.

As Frankish influence spread, so did the ordeal. During the reign of Charlemagne (768–814 A.D.) the ordeal was elaborated dramatically. New forms were invented, their use spread widely, and official (governmental) reliance on them increased dramatically (Bartlett, 1986:9). Charlemagne's father Pippin had relied on the ordeal of the cross. Charlemagne introduced this form of ordeal by decree into Italian, Ripurian, Salic, and Saxon law. However, it was banned by Lewis the Pious in 818 as sacrilegious—a mockery of Christ's crucifixion. Other types of ordeals, however, fared better. Many introduced during the reign of Charlemagne were in popular use well into the thirteenth century—most notably the ordeal of hot water described at the outset of the chapter.

The ordeal of cold water, for instance, resolved disputes by casting an individual into the water. The accused, whose hands and feet were bound, either sank or floated. On the premise that pure water would not receive the body of an unholy individual, those who floated were deemed guilty while those who sank like a stone were adjudged innocent.

The ordeal of the hot iron was also a Carolingian innovation. The accused carried either a bar or ball of red-hot iron seven paces. The hand was then wrapped and sealed. The healing of the hand was examined after 3 days. A "clean" heal—free of very serious injury or infection—revealed innocence. A similar ordeal required the accused to walk over red-hot plowshares, barefoot.

The various ordeals employed in the late eighth and early ninth centuries were elaborations of local customs or inventions of the spreading empire. Localities differed in the ordeals used and the type of evidence required to convict. For example, the ordeal of hot water required a "miracle" to *acquit* the accused (no serious burns) while the ordeal of cold water required a miracle to *convict* (a bound person floating in water). Some communities relied heavily on ordeals while others hardly ever used them. But "By the mid-ninth century all the ordeals of fire and water had come into vigorous life" (Bartlett, 1986:11).

Applications of ordeals occurred in a variety of contexts. Occasionally, political disputes of significant dimensions were resolved this way. In 859, King Lothar, husband to the barren Queen Tuetberga, accused his wife of sexual offenses in his attempt to get rid of her, marry his mistress, and legitimize their offspring. The queen had one of her servants undergo the ordeal of hot water. His success at the ordeal meant that King Lothar was unable to marry his mistress and his line became extinct. A century later (943) the count of Flanders, who had arranged the killing of the duke of Normandy, sought to dissuade the king of France from retaliating by offering to undergo the trial of fire to prove his innocence in the affair. The *offer, alone,* was enough to convince the king that the count was not guilty (Bartlett, 1986:15). These two examples illustrate how ordeals were sometimes ordered by the politically powerful in the pursuit of their ends, but sometimes they were volunteered by those accused as a means to clear their names.

More common were ordeals directed at resolving charges of sexual misalliances. Both males and females were required when charged with serious sex crimes (adultery, bestiality, incest, sodomy) to submit to the ordeal of the hot iron. So, too, questions of descent and inheritance were referred to such resolution. "The practice of the ordeal for disputed paternity was very common, found, for example, in Spanish and German law as well as in Ireland, Normandy, and the North" (Bartlett, 1986:20).

The most conspicuous application of the ordeal occurred in the twelfth century with its adoption as a regular form of legal trial in cases of heresy. Bartlett compared the great fear of heresy at this time to the mood of witch persecution in the sixteenth and seventeenth centuries, or the McCarthy-era persecution of suspected communists in the 1950s. Those whose *beliefs* were suspect were routinely subjected to the ordeal, sometimes en masse. Rather than subject the suspected heretic to the ordeal of hot iron (a trial that required 3 days to reach a verdict) heretics were more often subjected to the ordeal of cold water because sinking or floating was immediately apparent. The "swimming" of heretics or witches (throwing suspects into the water) was still practiced as late as the eighteenth and nineteenth centuries in Europe and America.

The laws of medieval Europe are full of references to ordeals for a wide range of offenses. However, regardless of the particular offense, the ordeal was always used only as a last resort—only when other means of uncovering the truth failed. Other forms of proof coexisted with the ordeal and when they could be relied on, the ordeal was not used. The main alternative to the ordeal was sworn testimony, or an oath. Another was the use of compurgators (those who would vouch for the truth of the claimant's cause). But *when human testimony could not be trusted, the ordeal was used.*

One very common situation of this sort occurred when there was no accuser or witness. When an individual was suspected of some crime and there was no person willing to bring the accusation, the suspect could clear his name in an ordeal. Indeed, the suspect would be required to undergo an ordeal if his sworn oath could not be accepted. Those whose word *was* accepted as proof were typically those of *higher status.* But more generally, the alternative of clearing one's name by oath (rather than ordeal) was reserved for those with good reputations. "The laws of Canute make a distinction between 'trustworthy men of good repute, who have never failed in oath or ordeal', who are allowed to clear themselves by their own oath; 'untrustworthy men', who require compurgators; and untrustworthy men who cannot find compurgators—this last group go to the ordeal" (Bartlett, 1986:31).

The most obvious group for whom the oath were not permitted were foreigners (i.e., strangers). "When juristic standing depended upon one's position in a web of kindred ties, bonds of lordship and dependency, blood status, and ethnic-territorial identity, the stranger was adrift. He hardly had an identity in legal terms. The Ripurian code orders that if a foreigner 'cannot find co-jurors in the Ripurian province, then he must clear himself by cauldron or lot'. In English law there are frequent references to the ordeal as the proof appropriate to 'the foreigner or friendless man'" (Bartlett, 1986:32).

In sum, the use of ordeals was widespread during the Medieval era throughout Europe. They coexisted with other forms of proof, but were used whenever these other forms could not be trusted. Individuals subjected to ordeals, in other words, were those whose word, itself, was not sufficient. Those whose reputations were *unknown or suspect* were required to validate their claims by resort to ordeals. The issues submitted to ordeals shared a common trait—they were cases that *had* to be decided. "The faithfulness of a wife, the falsity of a monk's doctrines, the unresolved theft where all suspicions pointed to one man: these had to go to trail, to judgment. This was the role of the ordeal. It was a device for dealing with situations in which certain knowledge was impossible but uncertainty was intolerable" (Bartlett, 1986:33). Situations that could not be permitted to go unresolved but for which no human method existed to effect a resolution were candidates for the ordeal. "The ordeal is entered into under conditions where the human group has usually reached deadlock. An ordeal is a tacit 'defusing' of the issue. It is not a judgement *by* God; it is a remitting of a case *ad judicium Dei*, 'to the judgement of God'" (Brown,1982:313).

Widespread until the thirteenth century, the ordeal was rarely used at all by courts by 1300. Historians have offered many explanations for the demise of the legal ordeal (see Bartlett, 1986, Chapters 4 and 5). The most convincing explanation focuses on religious objections to the practice. The ordeal was seen as wrong because it ordered God to respond to the demands of humans. By the twelfth century, canon law was significantly more important in the maintenance of law and order than it had ever been before. Questions about the legitimacy of the ordeal came to be voiced frequently in the codification of such laws. Was the ordeal to be canonical law? Some popes had been equivocal while others had openly opposed their use. The virtual absence of reference to ordeals in the Bible also made the practice suspect (only one passage, in Numbers, refers to an ordeal—that of Bitter Waters for a wife suspected of infidelity). The ordeal, in short, was not supported by Biblical or other religious sources.

In the course of the twelfth century, the practice came increasingly to be viewed as a secular superstition. It was also condemned as "tempting God" or demanding a miracle. Twelfth-century metaphysics held that mortals could not, or at least should not command God to reveal His purpose. In the latter twelfth and early thirteenth centuries, priests were increasingly forbidden to become involved in ordeals. In 1215 Pope Gregory IX completely forbade any priestly involvement in ordeals. The ordeal was then gradually abandoned as a form of sacred or secular trial. By the end of the century, it was employed only rarely.

As ordeals disappeared as a form of proof, other forms gained in popularity. The sworn oath had always been one alternative to an ordeal. And when an oath could be corroborated by witnesses, such evidence was sufficient. In the absence of witnesses, compurgators (character witnesses) could attest to the good reputation of the accused. While compurgation had long been an alternative to ordeals, once the practice of trial by ordeal was condemned, compurgation became a primary form of proof (Bartlett, 1986:136). Relatedly, in the course of the thirteenth century, the trial jury emerged in a few regions (in England and Denmark).

The dominant form of proof that replaced the ordeal, however, was torture, a practice sanctioned by Roman law and consistent with the growing inquisitorial nature of judicial practice.

> Until that period (the twelfth and thirteenth centuries) both criminal and civil cases had usually been raised and pursued by the injured party; the court then decided which proof should apply; and the accuser could suffer if the case went against him. With the development of inquisitorial techniques, officers of Church and State began to assume, to a much greater degree, the right to initiate proceedings and to take a much more active role in the court. . . . Thus an active inquisitorial judge now confronted a suspect in circumstances which made it easy to probe, to intimidate, and to harry him. (Bartlett, 1986:140)

Since a conviction in the absence of two eye-witnesses required a confession (in Roman law), torture was frequently used to extract that proof. Indeed, judicial torture largely replaced the ordeal in the period 1200—1700 and was being applied in very similar circumstances (in cases of heresy, treason, or nocturnal offenses not seen by any witnesses). And, like the ordeal, torture was a last resort used only when other forms of proof were unavailable.

Ordeals were not entirely replaced by torture. Witchcraft and sorcery were still viewed as sufficiently hideous crimes to warrant special treatment, if not by judges, by the European populace. Judicial use of the ordeal of cold water was generally frowned on. But there is abundant evidence of "swimming" of witches (crowds throwing them, bound, into the water) throughout Europe even into the eighteenth century. Such a practice should be viewed as a survival of the ordeal of cold water. And in colonial Virginia, the ordeal of cold water was used by a court in 1706 (Burr, 1914).

As "irrational" or "superstitious" as ordeals may strike us today, that is not at all how they were viewed by contemporaries. It has been argued, for example, that an ordeal was as "open ended as a Rorschach test" permitting any outcome desired by the judge (Brown, 1982). Indeed, Brown insists that the ordeal served to build consensus in small communities by defusing the issue of guilt or innocence (placing it in God's, not humans' hand) and drawing out the entire process to permit widespread participation that determined the outcome. During the lengthy preparations for the ordeal (subjects were required to fast and pray for 3 days prior to being taken to the ordeal) there was ample time for contestants to resolve disputes. And if this failed, the ordeal was sufficiently ambiguous to permit the group to determine the outcome. The hand that was examined after 3 days could not, physically, be healed. As such, any judgment, Brown concludes, was *subjective* and reflected the sentiment of the community.

Brown argues that ordeals were not what they appeared—not forms of proof—but rather a mode of consensus building. In essence, Brown is arguing that an ordeal could not *really* be a form of proof. Therefore, it must have served some other function.

Ordeals probably do foster consensus. However, it is not true, as Brown argues, that they are not a form of proof. Ordeals did exactly what they appeared to do—they produced an unimpeachable verdict that was widely regarded as valid. In an historical era in which miracles were accepted as ordinary events and one characterized by a belief in immanent justice, the ordeal did just what it promised. As historian Charles Radding (1989) notes, the belief in immanent justice causes a view of natural phenomena as reward or punishment from God. Hail, pestilence, or virtually any unusual natural phenomenon were seen as a sign of God's judgment. The ordeal was no more or less astonishing than other godly manifestations. The elaborate rituals of the ordeal fit understandably within this world view. If properly done, and only if properly done, the ordeal ritual would result in the truth. The scrupulous attention to detail in such rituals attests to the belief that they were magical. Quite simply, *the ordeal gave a believable answer when humans could not be trusted to give one.* By sustaining or refuting an individual's claims about themselves, *they established or maintained reputations.* As such, *ordeals were a form of surveillance.*

What about the problem of validity? Did ordeals *actually* uncover malfeasance? Were they accurate? What evidence exists suggests that about half of those subjected to ordeals were exonerated (Lea, 1973:xxvi). But were the truly guilty convicted? Undoubtedly some were. And many of those accused of crimes confessed before submitting to an ordeal. "In those ages of faith, the professing Christian, conscious of guilt, must indeed have been hardened who could undergo these awful rites, pledging his salvation on his innocence, and knowing under such circumstances that the direct intervention of Heaven could alone save him from having his hand boiled to rags after which he was to meet the full punishment of his crime, and perhaps in addition lose a member for the perjury committed. With such a prospect, all motives would conspire to lead him to a prompt and frank acknowledgment in the early stages of the proceedings against him" (Lea, 1972:149).

But whether ordeals were more valid than juries, for example, is not important. What really matters is that the verdicts rendered by ordeals were believed. There was rarely any attempt to appeal the verdict. Despite what popes or priests may have thought about "tempting God," there seems to have been little doubt in the minds of average people that the truth had been revealed.

For my purposes, the ordeal must be seen as a form of surveillance; a means of establishing or maintaining a reputation, especially among *strangers*. As noted earlier, foreigners were especially likely to be subjected to ordeals. And as Arthur Howland notes in his introduction to Henry Lea's "The Ordeal," "The ordeal itself indicates a decreasing reliance upon kin and friends and an increasing reluctance to accept traditional kin solidarity on the part of a society in the process of shaping new and wider social bonds" (Lea, 1972:xxvi).

The distribution of ordeals gives some clues to the conditions associated with its use. Tribal files contained in The Human Relations Area Files were examined by anthropologist John M. Roberts in 1965. He was interested in describing the types of societies that relied on oaths, on ordeals, and on both. His research showed ordeals to be more common in *larger communities,* those with intermediate or *high political integration,* high degrees of *economic complexity,* and more elaborate forms of *jurisdictional hierarchy.* Most interestingly, when Roberts considered child socialization strategies, he found

> the most interesting relationships are those associating obedience training with the presence of ordeals and responsibility training with the presence of oaths. . . . Both ordeals and oaths then are linked with anxiety. The former is associated with obedience and the latter with responsibility training. . . . Oaths, of course, appear to be simpler than ordeals. Very importantly . . . oaths have persisted into modern industrial society, albeit in an attenuated form, whereas ordeals in their traditional forms have disappeared. (Roberts, 1965:204–205).

"Responsibility" and "obedience" are terms coined by researchers Bacon, Barry, and Child to describe broad differences in forms of child-rearing. "An extreme of responsibility in this sense would be found in the *willing* performance of *laborious* duties or tasks, which the child has come to carry out on his own at the proper time and can be trusted to do. It can be contrasted with high obedience, where the child may passively do what he is told on any occasion, but has not himself learned to perform duties without immediate instruction" (Bacon, Barry, and Child, 1952, cited in Roberts, 1965). Another way of phrasing this difference might be to say that responsibility is conformity without constant supervision whereas obedience is conformity as a result of supervision. Alternatively, we might focus on responsibility as enforced by the possibility of internal feelings of *guilt* and obedience as enforced by the possibility of *shame*. If these parallels may be drawn, we might then say that oaths were found in cultures closer to the "guilt" end and ordeals in cultures closer to the "shame" end of the guilt–shame continuum. Or, as Roberts speculates; "It can be suggested, then, that oaths are effective in the cultures which have responsibility training and appropriate gods and that they will not be effective in cultures which lack the appropriate antecedent psychological training for them" (Roberts, 1965:206).

Such an interpretation clearly accords with the observation that oaths have persisted into modern times whereas ordeals are not a conspicuous part of our legal apparatus. But all this rests on the presumption that certain cultures do not rely on ordeals.

It can certainly be shown that many cultures, in fact, do not include ordeals in their legal codes. But no amount of responsibility training can socialize individuals to conform completely. Oaths and other forms of social control that rely on a clear knowledge and trust of the one making the claim will almost never suffice. There will always be circumstances when the word of an individual cannot be taken as truth, where there is a reasonable presumption of guilt without any objective evidence to support or refute such suspicions. It is under these conditions that ordeals are found, as they always have been. However, ordeals may exist alongside other legal forms of proof and not be embodied in the legal code.

The argument that I wish to develop is that modern-day American society is full of ordeals. By this I mean that there are numerous occasions where an individual, suspected of having compromised his or her claims or statements, is subjected to a ritual trial in which the results are revealed by some higher, nonhuman agency. The main difference between ordeals of the Middle Ages and those of today is in who or what is called on to render the truthful decision. God was the source of truth for judges in medieval times whereas *science*—or at least the appearance of it—is now called on to do the same thing. The appeal to science to uncover deception has a long and interesting history.

In the rest of this chapter I will describe several ordeals that have arisen this century to uncover deception. My focus will be on preemployment tests and trials. The reason I do this is because employment tests are directed, primarily, at individuals in their early twenties—those most likely to be emancipated. Unfortunately, there are very few reliable sources of information on the administration of employment tests that would permit an historical comparison of their use. It is not possible to determine, for example, what percentage of young applicants for employment were subjected to lie detector tests 40 years ago. There are some data, collected from employers, for the 1971–1991 era. To the extent possible, I will rely on this information to investigate whether the use of employment tests has grown or declined in response to the changes in rates of emancipation. Keep in mind that emancipation is only one manifestation of being a "stranger." Increases in youthful emancipation have been accompanied by significant increases in many other types of solitary living, migration, and other social changes that make reputations unknown or ambiguous. Changes in federal and state law, for example, may now prohibit certain forms of discrimination. If an employer is not permitted to refuse to hire those she or he distrusts (e.g., blacks, women), then people will be hired who have ambiguous reputations. Employment tests and other forms of ordeals (just like credentials) are one response to that ambiguity. The employment tests I will consider include lie detector, drug, and honesty tests. Each is a ritual trial that renders a verdict based on an appeal to a nonhuman agency and each is now (or recently) widely used.

The Lie Detector Test

The ancient Hindus employed an ordeal that required the suspect to chew a mouthful of rice that had been blessed in a ritual and then spit it out on a leaf of the sacred Pipal tree. The one who could spit out all the rice was considered innocent. But should rice stick to the tongue or palate, the accused was judged guilty (Lykken, 1981:26). A similar European ordeal known as the *corsnaed* required the accused to swallow a piece of barley bread that had been elaborately consecrated in a religious ceremony. Guilt or innocence was determined by the ability of the accused to swallow (Lea, 1973:93–94). Even the simple administration of the Christian Eucharist communion wafer has served as an ordeal in the past. The presumption underlying all such ordeals was that a guilty person would be unable to swallow because God would not allow it.

It is well known that people show physiological signs of lying. The lie may be accompanied by altered speech patterns, changes in posture, fidgeting, coughing, or other signs of discomfort. In the late nineteenth century, a number of criminologists and psychologists began studies of how people react to their own lying. The underlying assumption of all such research was that there is an *objective deception reaction*—a regular and measurable response to lying. The great Italian criminologist Cesare Lombroso was the first to report having used a machine to detect lying (1895). Lombroso and his student Mosso used a plethysmograph, a device for measuring changes in the volume of a limb, to record pulse and blood pressure changes of subjects during interrogation. Other late 19th century researchers pursued similar strategies. Russian psychologist A.R. Luria studied finger tremors and reaction time during interrogation of criminal suspects. Sir Francis Galton (cousin to Charles Darwin) studied word association. He would have suspects respond to a series of words by giving the first word that came to mind. Guilty suspects would take longer to respond to words associated with the crime than innocent subjects (presumably, the guilty person would need time to think of a nonincriminating response to words that normally would evoke guilty associations). Harvard psychology professor Hugo Munsterberg, in 1908, published his review of all such lie detection strategies in his book *On the Witness Stand*. Mursterberg's student William M. Marston claimed to have discovered a lie response in 1915 when he demonstrated that systolic blood pressure changes were associated with deception. He is credited with coining the term "lie detector" for devices that measured physiological responses to questions.

Marston championed the use of lie detectors widely and made extravagant claims for their usefulness and validity in his 1938 book *The Lie Detector Test*. Reports by Marston appeared in popular magazines such as *Look* along with full-page advertisements for the service. An article in the December 6, 1938 issue of *Look* magazine "described his use of the polygraph in marital counseling; a wife's reaction to her husband's kiss is compared with her response to the kiss of an attractive stranger" (Lykken, 1981:27). Marston's claims about the usefulness of the test and his entrepreneurial zeal were met with skepticism and condemnation by serious researchers. But police officials and the general public were obviously impressed with this new ordeal—a means for *scientifically* uncovering truth struck Americans as a tremendous advance.

Influenced by Marston's work, August Vollmer, chief of the Berkeley Police Department in California, had John Larson, a member of his force, assemble the first continuous-recording interrogation polygraph in 1921. Vollmer relied on his new device in a number of criminal investigations with unexpectedly good results. Larson's device was soon miniaturized and its use spread rapidly among law enforcement agencies in America. Yet despite the growing popularity of the device, only one study of its validity was conducted. In 1938, Larson examined 62 suspects, whose records were then independently evaluated by nine psychologists. The number of subjects classified as deceptive ranged from 5 to 33, although 61 of the 62 suspects were, in fact, truthful (Lykken, 1981:29). His research was published that year in an article concluding "there is no disturbance graphic or in quantitative physiological terms specific for deception" (Larson, 1938:897). In short, Larson showed that there is no consistent, objective deception response. Larson's study was the only scientific one of the accuracy of the polygraph for almost 40 years after 1915 when Marston's lie detector first caught the imagination of law enforcement officials (Lykken, 1981:29).

Despite the absence of *scientific* evidence to substantiate the claims of polygraphers, the lie detector was immensely popular. Two of Larson's associates on the Berkeley police force, C.D. Lee and Leonarde Keeler, developed a portable polygraph and a set of written instructions for its use. Keeler went on to found a polygraph school in Chicago. The Keeler school and another in Chicago (established by competing polygrapher John Reid) were responsible for developing the technology and methodology that are now used in polygraph examinations (Barland, 1988). The development and dissemination of the lie detector were not done by scientists. Keeler had no professional psychological or scientific training, and Larson was a policeman. Marston, though he held a Ph.D. in psychology from Harvard, could not be called a scientist by the standards of the time, much less those of today. The study of the relationship between physiological and psychological responses is the field of psychophysiology. Few polygraphers today have training in this field of psychology and none did in the days of its development (Lykken, 1981:43).

In 1939, Paul Trovillo, a forensic psychologist with the Scientific Crime Detection laboratory (originally a unit of Northwestern University Law School, later a unit of the Chicago Police Department), wrote an overview paper for the highly respected *Journal of Criminal Law and Criminology* (a publication of Northwestern University law school). In his history of lie detection, Trovillo (1939:vol 39:850, vol 40:111) notes that

> the historical accounts of deception-detecting from the days of Christ, through the Middle Ages, are the history of the Ordeal. The ordeal technique is not based on any peculiar insight into the psychological processes underlying awareness of guilt. Rather, it arises out of superstition and religious faith. Nowadays one would give little credence to such miraculous tales. . . . It is possible today, for objective investigation of deception, to utilize many different techniques and approaches.

Clearly, Trovillo found in the "new" polygraphic techniques a dramatic advance over the ordeals of the Middle Ages because the former relied on the *science* of psychology. The assumption that deception was mirrored in physiological responses that could be objectively and scientifically measured was the basis for the polygraph. Yet there was no scientific evidence that this could, in fact, be done. Psychology in the first half of the century actually offered little to connect emotion and physical response. As recently as 1986, the American Psychological Association adopted a resolution stating that scientific evidence for the effectiveness of polygraph tests was unsatisfactory, a conclusion unanimously adopted by the APA Council of Representatives after more than a year of study by two separate panels (Douglas, Feld, and Asquith, 1989:13–16).

After a thorough review of all pertinent literature, Lykken (1981) estimated that a total of only 80 scientific articles had, between 1900 and 1980, been written about the polygraph. Hundreds of others have been written by advocates or vendors in nonscientific outlets. The U.S. Congress Office of Technology Assessment in 1983 reported that "The Office of Technology Assessment concluded that the available research evidence does not establish the scientific validity of the polygraph for [personnel screening] purposes. . . . When used in criminal investigations, the polygraph test detects deception better than chance, but with error rates that could be considered significant" (U.S. Congress, Office of Technology Assessment, 1983:5).

Today, the standard polygraph has three components. First is a sphygmomanometer that is wrapped around the upper arm. This records changes in blood pressure. Second, two tubes are wrapped around the upper and lower chest. These record changes in respiration. Third, two electrodes attached to the index and second finger of one hand record changes in the electrical conductivity (altered by perspiration) of the skin. These three instruments record their measurements continuously on a paper chart. The polygraph examiner relies on this chart to form an opinion about the likelihood of deception. Generally speaking, it is assumed that deceptive answers will produce a different pattern of responses than a truthful one.

The polygraph test is conducted in three stages. First there is a pretest interview. The examiner introduces him or herself and explains the testing procedure and the instrument. Basic information is obtained: name, birth date, marital status, number of children, and so forth. The examiner then explains the reason for the questions that will be asked. Every question that will be asked during the test is read and rehearsed. For example, the examiner might tell the subject that he will ask the question "From the time you graduated from high school up to two years ago, did you ever steal anything of value? Would you be able to answer 'NO' to that?" Should the respondent object that virtually no person could answer that question truthfully by saying 'NO', the examiner will attempt to reword the question. He might, for example, say "I'm just trying to get a wording that you're comfortable with. It's just a matter of choosing a figure. What sort of figure would you like to have me use in this question?" (Lykken, 1981:14). Once all questions have been read and rehearsed in this fashion, the actual test begins.

The examiner will ask the respondent a series of questions that can be answered Yes or No. One variety of the test poses a series of questions that contains relevant information about the subject matter being tested (Have you ever stolen as much as $50 from an employer?) but that is interspersed among a series of neutral questions (Is today Monday?). If the responses are stronger to the relevant questions than to the neutral ones, the person is diagnosed a being deceptive. In another variant, a series of "control" questions is asked that is vague and refers to things almost everyone has done in their lifetime (as in the example above). These questions are designed to force the individual to be more concerned with them than with the relevant ones so that the latter will generate a stronger physiological response. If responses to relevant questions are stronger than to control questions, the subject is judged to be deceptive.

The third stage of the test—the posttest interview—begins after the polygraph examination is completed. The examiner will describe results to certain questions that might suggest deception.

> On the questions about [for example, stealing], I'm getting reactions. I'm wondering if there is anything about those questions that might account for what I'm getting? Anything about the way they're worded? Maybe something about some previous experience with something stolen from your office or some currency you might have taken some other time? In other words, is there anything you haven't already told me about that might explain why you're reacting this way to these questions? I tell you what, I'm going to give you a few minutes to collect yourself and maybe you'll think of some reason why I'm getting these reactions. You just sit there quietly and think about it and I'll be back in a few minutes.

On returning, the examiner will ask if there is anything else the subject wants to say. If not, he or she may be asked to take the entire test again (Lykken, 1981:21–22).

The scientific accuracy of the components of the polygraph are not problematic. A sphygmomanometer is regarded as an accurate method for recording changes in blood pressure. So too with the other components. Each is a scientifically validated method for measuring the physiological reactions it is supposed to. The problem with the polygraph is that there is no evidence that these physiological changes are unique to deception. As the U.S. Senate noted in 1987, "Anger, fear, anxiety, surprise, shame, embarrassment and resentment are some of the psychological states which can cause identical changes. At best, the polygraph can claim to measure changes indicative of stress; but neither the machine nor the examiner can distinguish whether deception or another state of mind caused the stressed response with an acceptable degree of certainty" (U.S. Senate, 1987:41).

Despite the lack of scientific support or evidence for the validity of the polygraph, its proponents trust it and endorse its use. The FBI published a position paper on the polygraph in 1980. It is characterized as "a highly sophisticated, scientifically based technique." Although only one study is cited to support these claims, the FBI concludes "The polygraph technique, when properly used by competent, well-trained examiners, possesses a high degree of accuracy. . . it can eliminate suspects, verify witnesses' statements, corroborate informant information, and determine the veracity of a complainant's statement" (Federal Bureau of Investigation, 1980).

In 1987, over two million polygraph tests were administered by private employers, 70 percent of which were for preemployment purposes, 15 percent in random postemployment screening, and only 15 percent as part of an investigation of a specific incident relating to the employer (U.S. Senate, 1987:46).

Why has the polygraph been so popular? What makes a scientifically useless test acceptable to employers and law-enforcement agents? The most plausible answer is that it works—*despite* the fact that the lie detector cannot accurately distinguish between truth and deception. Support for such a conclusion may be found in statements like the following (from the FBI position paper on the polygraph): "The polygraph. . . can dramatically increase the conviction rate due to the high occurrence of confessions made by suspects who had been less than candid prior to the polygraph examinations" (FBI, 1980:5). The third stage of the polygraph examination is done with the machine turned off. During this interview, the tester will repeatedly probe in an apparent attempt to resolve "reactions" found during the examination. Usually, however, there are no reactions and the probing is done regardless of the results of the polygraph test. Such probing is done in such a way to encourage a confession—to give the subject an opportunity to admit to something not even hinted at by the examination. "For many polygraphers, the post-test interrogation and the confession it so often induces is the real object of the whole exercise" (Lykken, 1981:207). In fact, the *majority* of individuals tested by polygraph make some form of damaging admission. Among job applicants, it is estimated that three-quarters admit to some past offense (Lykken, 1981:206). Why?

We might ask the same thing of the ordeal of hot iron or boiling water. "There can be little doubt that it [the ordeal] was frequently found to be of use in extorting confession or unwilling testimony. The elaborate nature of the ritual employed, with its impressive adjurations and exorcisms, was well fitted to excite the imagination and alarm the conscience" (Lea, 1973:149). If a subject believes that the ordeal works, whether it be a polygraph machine or a mouth of dry bread, there is strong incentive for the guilty to confess. The ritual aspects of a polygraph ordeal (the pretest interview, the connections of electrodes and straps to the body, the careful repetition of questions over and over) serve the same purpose as the requiem mass celebrated before an ordeal of hot water. The ritual sensitizes subjects—it frightens them. It helps convince them that there is no hope of fooling the ordeal. It makes lying seem senseless. If they believe in the ordeal, *the guilty are prone to confess.*

In his book on the subject, Lykken recounts anecdotes of police officers who interrogate gullible subjects by wrapping the cord to the police cruiser radio microphone around a suspect's arm. When the suspect responds to a question, the officer pushes the "transmit" button and tells the subject, "See that red light on the dash—that means you're lying. Now, come on and tell us the truth." He also recounts a story of a team of officers who placed a sheet of paper in a copying machine that had the words "HE IS LYING" typed on it. The suspect was told that the machine was a "truth verifier." During an interrogation officers would push the copy button whenever they doubted the suspect's story. Out would come a page with the verdict as to the veracity of the answer given. That such tricks work is evidence of how effective any ordeal can be *when it is trusted.*

And the polygraph *is* (or has been) trusted despite the fact that it has no scientific basis. But neither did medieval ordeals (although fear could make the hand more sensitive to burning or the mouth dryer). But validity is hardly the issue when it comes to ordeals. As a form of surveillance, ordeals "work." One way they work is by discouraging deviance—they are a form of deterrence. They also elicit confessions. Ordeals maintain reputations. The honest person has no reason to refuse a polygraph examination. By it, she may maintain her good name. Ordeals also establish reputations. The guilty person might confess his misdeeds and subsequently be branded a thief, liar, or worse.

In 1987, the U.S. Congress passed the Polygraph Protection Act. This act outlawed the use of polygraphs by employers for preemployment screening or random testing. The purpose of this federal law "is to eliminate the denial of employment opportunities by prohibiting the least accurate yet more widely used lie-detector tests, pre-employment and random examinations, and providing standards for and safeguards from abuse during tests not prohibited" (U.S. Senate, 1987:39). As noted in the text of the law, "Many experts agree that fear of the machine is an essential element necessary to obtain confessions. One noted examiner claimed the polygraph to be 'the best confession-getter since the cattle-prod'. But it is this intentional use of fear and intimidation which disturbs many of the opponents of the test." (U.S. Senate, 1987:42). Congress based its conclusion on research conducted by the Office of Technology Assessment. They outlawed the polygraph except in cases of specific, ongoing investigations of crime in the workplace. The basis of this law was the absence of any *scientific* evidence about the validity of the test. Scientific evidence finally caught up with the advocates of the polygraph ordeal. Although the test may have worked, it worked for the wrong reasons. Moreover, it did not always work. And when it failed, it almost always labeled as deceptive an honest person.

In Medieval times, the doubtful submitted their unanswerable questions to God for a definitive answer. Ultimately, however, God's emissary (the Pope) said that answers could not be given that way. So too in modern times. The doubtful have submitted their unanswerable questions to science for a definitive answer. But with respect to lie detectors scientists determined that answers could not be given that way.

But the arsenal of ordeals available to employers is vast and having lost the polygraph did not seriously jeopardize the scientific quest for truth verifiers. Employers valued the lie detector. After it was outlawed alternative methods of checking people's claims about themselves were developed.

Integrity Testing

Employers have turned increasingly, of late, to a new form of truth verification—the so-called "honesty/integrity test." Approximately 6,000 business establishments in the United States are now estimated to use honesty/integrity tests in the process of screening and selecting job applicants for employment (U.S. Congress, Office of Technology Assessment, 1990a) About 3.5 million such tests were given in 1988 (Douglas et al., 1989:142). Virtually all such tests (95 percent) are used in pre-employment screening rather than among current employees. And they are expected to gain in popularity because of the legal prohibition against the use of the polygraph for pre-employment screening .

Integrity tests are all proprietary. Each of the 10 major firms that sells the tests has developed its own inventory. Many integrity tests were, in fact, developed or commissioned by polygraphers for use in states where polygraph use was restricted (Sackett, Burris, and Callahan, 1989:496). The scientific community of psychologists has not, as a whole, been involved in the development of these tests. Publishers advertise their products as having been developed by psychologists on their staff. However, the proprietary nature of the for-profit integrity tests makes them largely unavailable for scrutiny by psychologists who do not work for the publishers. Whether or not integrity tests conform to acceptable scientific standards for psychological personality inventories is an unanswered question—and likely to remain so.

Unlike the polygraph, integrity tests are paper and pencil examinations that often resemble personality profiles in their form. The Congressional

Office of Technology Assessment defines such tests as "written tests designed to identify individuals. . . who have relatively high propensities to steal money or property on the job, or who are likely to engage in behavior of a more generally 'counterproductive' nature. Counterproductivity in this context often includes types of 'time theft', e.g., tardiness, sick leave abuse, and absenteeism" (U.S. Congress, Office of Technology Assessment, 1990a:1). Such tests are scored in such a way to render a very simple result: recommend/not acceptable. The typical "passing" rate (scoring as "trustworthy") is between 40 and 70 percent. This means that typically half of job applicants will "fail" (Sackett et al., 1989:522).

But just like the polygraph, integrity tests are used most frequently among applicants who are *less easily screened*—those who do not have recognized educational or other credentials. Thus, it is nonmanagerial, less-skilled job applicants such as those for convenience store employees or retail clerks who are most often asked to submit to such tests. Employers are motivated to use paper and pencil honesty tests for the same reason they are motivated to use the polygraph: *the uncertainty in hiring strangers who lack known reputations raises legitimate fears that costly mistakes may be made in hiring.* A dishonest employee who handles the cash register is in a position to cost an employer significant profits. Very reliable evidence of employee theft exists and suggests that it is widespread. One study of over 9,000 employees in retail trades found that one-third admitted to some type of theft (Hollinger and Clark, 1983) .

It is the sense of widespread theft and other forms of "counterproductive" behaviors that fosters the desire to use truth verifiers. Stated differently, it is widespread *distrust* of potential employees that leads to the use of these methods. If one makes the assumption that theft (or any form of deviance) is caused or can be predicted by something as simple as a *personality* trait—that there are inherently dishonest and inherently honest people—then identifying the dishonest employee is seen as a possible solution to deviance in the workplace. If, on the other hand, theft and counterproductive behaviors are thought to be caused by larger organizational or sociological factors, then personality assessments offer little hope of countering the problem.

These tests are typically the final hurdle in the preemployment screening process. As such, they resemble other ordeals that are employed as a last resort. Only after the applicant has gone through the entire screening process for ability and job experiences is he or she given an honesty test (Sackett et al., 1989:532). Having found a candidate who otherwise qualifies for a job, the employer resorts to one last test. No matter how much past experience, or how ideally suited for the actual job a candidate may appear, there is always doubt about character when the applicant is a *stranger.* Who knows, maybe this candidate lied about his or her experience? Perhaps references were fabricated. Lacking *personal* knowledge to the contrary, the employer will be uncertain about whether to trust a person applying for a job. The hallmark of all ordeals is that they give a *conclusive answer when uncertainty is intolerable.* It is the intolerable uncertainty in hiring that led to the invention and subsequent use of these tests.

Two forms of integrity tests are now marketed. The *overt integrity test* includes questions designed to measure attitudes about specific forms of dishonesty and past involvement in such behaviors (e.g., theft). Questions such as "How honest are you?" "How often do you tell the truth?" "How prompt are you?" or "Do you think it is stealing to take small items home from work?" are typical for this type of test. The other type of test, the *personality-based* or *veiled purpose test,* is more like a standard personality inventory. Such tests typically include no overt references to theft or obvious deviance on the job. They measure a range of attitudes and values presumably related to honesty, integrity, and conformity. Questions such as "How often do you blush?" "How often do you make your bed?" "Are you an optimist?" and "How often are you embarrassed?" are typical for this type of test (U.S. Congress, Office of Technology Assessment, 1990a:2). In recent years, the veiled purpose personality test has become much more popular as these tests have been broadened to include a wide range of personality traits.

The use of psychological personality inventories in preemployment screening is nothing new. At least since the beginning of the century, industry has relied on various paper and pencil tests to select employees. Intelligence tests originally developed at the turn of the century and employed by the military to recruit and assign soldiers in both World Wars have enjoyed a certain degree of popularity among employers since. But the emphasis on measuring honesty or integrity as components of unchanging personality is much greater today than in the recent past when polygraphs were legal. Still, the integrity test is best viewed as an extension of a long-standing practice: the use of psychological personality assessments for preemployement screening. In fact, one integrity test publisher argued that there is no fundamental conceptual difference between integrity tests and other personality tests (U.S. Congress, Office of Technology Assessment, 1990a:36).

The unanswered question about all such tests, regardless of form, is how or why they could predict future behaviors. Tests that query about past dishonest acts, for example, are premised on the belief that people continue to act pretty much the same way over time. Further, it must be assumed that admissions of past acts are a reasonable surrogate for *actual* past acts. But if a person truthfully admits to past acts of deviance, they are, in fact, reporting *honestly.* Here the honest individual would be likely to "fail" an integrity test (though such a person might be inclined to theft if thievery is a personality trait). On the other hand, should an individual deny past dishonesty, thereby appearing to be a better risk, such claims may actually be evidence of *dishonesty*. Here the dishonest individual would be more likely to "pass" an integrity test. Finally, and most importantly, if admissions of past dishonesty are useful in predicting future dishonesty, why not simply ask applicants, straightforwardly, about past acts of deviance? Why subject them to a test? (U.S. Congress, Office of Technology Assessment, 1990a:34). The answer, of course, is that tests have the imprimatur of *science*—of psychology in this instance. But since professional psychologists have not been actively involved in the development or validation of such tests, it is not psychology that underlies the tests. It is rather the *appearance* of science—of pseudoscience. These tests *resemble* validated and established psychological inventories even though they are not.

The integrity test industry is very secretive about its product. The tests and scoring templates are proprietary, thereby ensuring that impartial, scientific studies of them are impossible. The producers claim that integrity test scores are valid predictors of future dishonesty or "counterproductive" behaviors on the job. Validity and reliability studies of such tests have been conducted by the publishers themselves. These studies show that the correlation between scores on honesty tests and other measures of dishonesty (self reports of thefts, absenteeism, termination, monthly inventory 'shrinkage' admissions during a polygraph exam, supervisor ratings) are actually quite low (correlations of .20 to .59) (Sackett et al., 1989:502–506). But no valid scientific study corroborates even these quite modest claims made about such tests. Integrity test scores have been compared with polygraph results and found to correlate rather well. However, the total absence of evidence to support the validity of polygraphy makes it an extremely poor criterion to use in establishing the validity of integrity tests.

Consider the following "evidence" offered in support of integrity tests. A total of 3,790 employees were given a test and hired regardless of their test performance. Subsequent investigations by management revealed that 91 employees had committed some type of theft. Among these 91, 75 had failed the integrity test and only 16 had passed it. Surely this "evidence" would appear to show that the test distinguished well between thieves and honest employees. However among the 3,699 for whom the investigation did not reveal any theft, 2,145 had also failed the test and 1,554 had passed. "Thus, 75 of those taking the test (2 percent of the total 3,790) are known to have been characterized correctly by the test and 16 are known to have been characterized incorrectly. What about the rest? If those 3,699 not detected as thieves are assumed to be honest, then 2,145 (58 percent) were misclassified; if a substantial number of them were

indeed thieves, the observed correlation between the test and the outcome measure could be higher, lower, or equal to the actual correlation"
(U.S. Congress, Office of Technology Assessment, 1990a:54).

The idea behind these tests is that honesty is a *personality trait* that does
not change dramatically from one situation or time to another. The authors of these inventories believe that a person who scores in the "doubtful honesty" range is, in fact, inherently dishonest regardless of the
circumstances. This assumption, however, is not one shared by most
professional psychologists. As noted by the Office of Technology Assessment in its evaluation of these tests:

> A very important question about workplace deviance is the relative
> effects of individual propensities, on the one hand, and characteris-
> tics of the work environment or situation, on the other. Although
> this is a specific instance of the debate between "traits and states"
> that continues to occupy psychological researchers, there appears to
> be widespread agreement that it is useful to discuss theft and
> workplace deviance with reference to situational as well as individ-
> ual variables. (U.S. Congress, Office of Technology Assessment,
> 1990a:29)

Integrity tests measure *only* individual traits. They ignore totally the
workplace norms that might sanction theft or the managerial structure
that might appear to do the same thing.

Based on their *scientific* merit only, integrity tests cannot be argued to be
effective. Indeed, the Office of Technology Assessment study of such tests
concluded "The research on integrity tests has not yet produced data that
clearly supports or dismisses the assertion that these tests can predict
dishonest behavior" (U.S. Congress, Office of Technology Assessment,
1990a:8). There is simply no reliable evidence on which to make a reasoned decision about whether these paper and pencil lie detectors actually detect lies or dishonesty or a propensity to be honest or dishonest.

As with any ordeal however, integrity tests might actually "work."
Even if unable to distinguish the honest from the dishonest individual
(i.e., if invalid) , or even if honesty is a situationally determined characteristic (i.e., if unreliable), honesty tests may actually reduce employee
deviance. That is, after all, their raison d'etre. After instituting a preemployment honesty testing policy, lower rates of "shrinkage" (inventory
losses that cannot be accounted for) have been noted (Sackett et al., 1989).
More extravagant claims for these tests are made by researchers who
work for the companies that publish them (for a review see Jones and
Terris, 1991). And when a company institutes such a policy, it implicitly
announces to its employees that it is taking the issue of theft (or other

counterproductive behaviors) more seriously. A test that is believed to be capable of identifying the culprit among employees has obvious deterrent potential. Those employees who might otherwise break company rules might think twice before doing so if they happen to believe their company's honesty tests could identify them. As noted by two experts on integrity testing:

> Companies using psychological honesty tests generally believe that they are effective because they screen out theft-prone individuals and screen in honest, productive employees. There are, however, other possible explanations that could explain a reduction in theft. One is that the use of a valid selection procedure creates an organizational climate unfavorable to theft. . . . Another possibility is that using an honesty test sends a message to all applicants and employees that the company cares about preventing theft and will do something about it. . . . A third possible explanation is that a selection system sensitizes the entire work force to these issues. Using a psychological test to screen out theft-prone applicants usually generates a great deal of discussion about theft in all levels of the organization. (Jones and Terris, 1991:48)

Of course, most such tests are applied only in preemployment situations. However, even here, potential hires who are likely to engage in counterproductive acts may be dissuaded from doing so if subjected to a test before being hired. Or, such people may be less likely to go through the entire preemployment process (if they apply at all) if they believe their misdeeds are likely to be discovered.

To return to a point made earlier, the reason for these questionable tactics is distrust of strangers. The employer is confronted with the difficult task of selecting among applicants those best suited to the firm and those who will make the greatest contribution. There is often a vast amount of information available about applicants—all manner of possible credentials and certifiable skills. Most nonmanagerial employees, however, lack a lengthy resume. Indeed, they may offer little, if any, evidence about their trustworthiness. Since this question is so central to the employer and has such tremendous implications for long-term performance of the firm, leaving it unanswered is intolerable. If there is no other person or persons who could provide evidence, the only possibility is to live with the uncertainty or appeal to a nonhuman agency for a verdict. An appeal to pseudoscience to provide an answer makes good sense from that perspective.

When Georg Simmel noted that a lie is rather unimportant in simple face-to-face societies, he was pointing to the fact that intimates have a very hard time tricking each other. If you and I see each other regularly and share a wide network of friends and associates, it would be quite difficult for either of us to lie in an important way—to deceive sufficiently for it to matter. But when people do not know one another, there is little to help them know whether a statement is true. The basic problem is that a lie is invisible because it is only a concept. So too, more generally, is dishonesty. It may be possible to see the *consequences* of dishonesty, but dishonesty itself is only a concept. One cannot touch, taste, feel, see, smell, or hear a dishonesty or a lie. They simply are not empirical. If humans cannot see these things, but worry that they may be there, some extrahuman device must be used.

The same is true of many forms of deviance. They are invisible almost all the time. But visible or not, deviance is undesirable. When we turn our attention to the "problem" of drug use, the complications of detecting an invisible problem are most obvious.

Drug Testing

In the current climate of hysteria surrounding drug use, little else could damage an individual's reputation so much as being labeled a drug abuser. Drugs and their effects are blamed for virtually everything wrong with America: poor (or excellent) performance of athletes, crime in the streets, failures in school, the spread of AIDS, high rates of infant mortality, the declining competitiveness of American business, and especially, poor performance on the job. Anyone who is known to use illegal drugs—indeed anyone thought to be "soft" on drugs—thereby becomes viewed as a co-conspirator in the dismantling of America.

The past 10 years have been witness to unprecedented attempts to control the drug use problem we face. Two Presidents have committed themselves to securing "drug-free" schools, cities, and workplaces. Federal courts have amended evidentiary rules to admit illegally obtained testimony for the prosecution of drug dealers. Three fraternity houses at the University of Virginia were seized by the federal government in 1991 because seven students each sold marijuana or hallucinogenic mushrooms in them. But the most dramatic assault in the war on drugs is the implementation of mandatory testing of employees' urine for evidence of past drug use. All *federal* employees may be subjected to urine testing as a result of President Reagan's 1986 Executive Order 12564. According to a national survey of employers conducted by the Bureau of Labor Statistics in 1990, almost half (46 percent) of all private employers now have urine testing programs in place. By comparison, only 6 percent did in 1983 (Hayge, 1991; see also Michigan State University, 1991). The vast majority of urine testing programs (85 percent) is directed at job *applicants* rather than current employees (Hayge, 1989: Table 4)

Unlike the other forms of ordeals I have been discussing, drug tests are quite new, dating back no more than 20 years or so. In the 1960s drug testing was used exclusively in clinical settings—especially in methadone maintenance and drug rehabilitation programs. By 1970, the U.S. Department of Defense introduced mandatory urine testing to detect heroin use among soldiers returning from the war in Vietnam. By 1980, law enforcement agencies were using urine testing in jails to monitor drug use. It was not until the early 1980s that mass screening for drugs was done, and then only by the military. The demand for drug testing that was created by the military led to the development (by private firms) of low-cost screening tests of minimal but acceptable (by employers' standards) accuracy.

The "war" on drugs of the late 1980s and early 1990s is certainly not the first such war. However, the target of this war is new. This one is aimed primarily at cocaine. Earlier wars on drugs focused on substances with more blatantly obvious effects on their users. In 1827 the American Society for the Promotion of Temperance was founded. The focus of this temperance movement was alcohol. In 1851 the first prohibition law was enacted in Maine and within 4 years 13 states had similar statutes. Those laws were repealed only to be replaced by comparable ones in the early twentieth century. The importation of smokable opium was banned in 1909 and the 1914 Harrison Act prohibited the sale of most over-the-counter narcotics. Another war on alcohol culminated in the passage of the 18th Amendment in 1919 outlawing the sale of alcoholic beverages (see: Ackerman, 1991:5 ff).

Although there is nothing new about a "war" on drugs, there is certainly nothing in history like the testing of urine in such a war. American society is almost always waging a crusade against one substance or another. Temperance movements rise and fall, and have done so for at least a century and a half. But the present war on drugs is the first to employ an ordeal to detect secret users. In this regard, drug tests are quite similar to medieval ordeals directed at heretics. It was often quite difficult to be certain who was or was not a heretic and only God could reveal the truth. Describing the twelfth century ordeals, Bartlett noted:

In the eyes of frightened orthodox contemporaries, heresy was an insidious international conspiracy, all the more disturbing for being so invisible. It was hard for Catholics to know if their neighbours were harbouring heretical thoughts. Normal judicial procedures were inadequate: only extreme measures, in this case the ordeal, would do. (Bartlett, 1989:23).

We may substitute the words "drug use" for "heresy" in the above quotation and recognize how similar are our methods and motives. "In the eyes of frightened contemporaries, drug use is an insidious international conspiracy. It is hard to know if your neighbors are drug users. Normal judicial procedures are inadequate." When President Ronald Reagan signed Executive Order 12564 in 1986 he ordered all federal agencies to "establish a program to test for the use of illegal drugs by employees in sensitive positions" [Executive Order 12564, Section 3 (a)]. Indeed, the *testing* component is the only significant part of this executive order. Illegal drugs, by definition, are illegal so there was little an Executive Order could do about enforcement of existing laws. Clearly, existing judicial practices were perceived by the President to be ineffective. Executive Order 12564 must be seen as a statement that *normal judicial procedures were inadequate: only extreme measures, in this case drug tests, would do.*

There is only one reason to test people for drug use and that is because *it is not readily apparent that the person uses drugs.* If drug use were visible, no test would be needed. "Some drug testing programs may be envisioned as substitutes for more direct evaluations of job performance" (Lo, 1991:193). But if drug use *is* invisible, what convinced the President (and most members of Congress) that we needed extraordinary methods to combat it? That is a question that has never been answered. President Reagan justified his order with the following rationale: "Drug use is having serious adverse effects upon a significant proportion of the national work force and results in billions of dollars of lost productivity each year. The use of illegal drugs, on or off duty, by Federal employees is inconsistent not only with the law-abiding behavior expected of all citizens, but also with the special trust placed in such employees as servants of the public" (Executive Order 12,564, Introduction). The President did not attempt to justify his order with actual evidence of a workplace problem. Indeed, such evidence is virtually nonexistent. As noted by the authors of a book on drug testing by the American Society of Clinical Pathologists, "Losses from decreased productivity and lower profits result from behaviors that are sometimes *hard to quantify:* reduction in normal work capacity, poor workmanship, and mistakes or damage to company property" (Decresce, Lifshitz, Ambre, Mazura, Tilson, and Cochran, 1989:2, emphasis added). Despite repeated claims that billions of dollars are lost because of drug-impaired workers each year, there is no solid evidence to support such a claim. Rather, those involved in the early stages of the war on drugs cited specific instances of known drug-related loss and injury: an Amtrak accident in 1987 caused by engineers under the influence of marijuana, the failure of an entire computer system for a national bank as a result of mistakes by a programmer under the influence of drugs, and similar incidents (see U.S. Senate, 1988:5).

The *actual* extent of drug use on the job, much less drug-related losses, is not known. One federal agency charged with waging the war on drugs is the National Institute on Drug Abuse. It conducts yearly national surveys to estimate the extent of drug use in America. Its data are the most reliable now available. Of course, there is a very legitimate question about whether people will admit to using drugs. Even though the NIDA relies on anonymous surveys, it is likely that some people will lie about their drug use. That means that surveys are likely to underestimate the actual illegal drug use in a population. In its most recent, anonymous, survey in 1990, NIDA queried 9,259 individuals drawn randomly to represent the entire household population of the United States (this excludes residents of institutions). The findings from this survey reveal that 6 percent of Americans used one or more illegal drugs at least once in the month before the survey. Marijuana was the most frequently used drug: approximately 5 percent of Americans used it in the month prior to the survey. Fewer than 1 percent of Americans used any other illegal drug in the preceding month. When examined by age group it is found that youths in the emancipated age group (age 18 to 25) have the highest incidence of illegal drug use in the past month—15 percent. Among those 26 to 34 approximately 10 percent report past month use. And among those 35 and over the figure is 3 percent. Comparable statistics for the use of *alcohol* in the past month are 63 percent for those 18 to 25, 64 percent for those 26 to 34, and 52 percent for those 35 and older. The NIDA survey did not ask about drug (or alcohol) use on the job.

Furthermore, drug use has been declining rapidly for at least 13 years—that is, since long before the current "war on drugs" began. Compared to the 15 percent of 18 to 25 year olds who used drugs in 1990, the 1979 survey showed that more than twice that percent (37 percent) of 18 to 25 year olds admitted having used at least one illegal drug at least once in the past month. Similar declines were found for all other age groups (National Institute on Drug Abuse, 1991).

There is, unquestionably, a sizable minority of youths who use illegal drugs. Whether they use them at work or whether off work use affects on-the-job performance is not known. But fear that they might is one of the driving forces behind the current explosion in drug testing of job applicants. As President Reagan noted in his executive order, drug use *off* the job is not to be tolerated, either. Drug tests are especially good at detecting past, off-the-job use. Indeed, the tests presently used are not capable of indicating when the substance was ingested.

The Tests

The most commonly used drug tests are designed to detect evidence of a number of substances in *urine*, typically amphetamines, barbiturates, benzodiazepines (e.g., Valium or Librium), cannabinoids (marijuana, hashish), cocaine (and crack), methaqualone (quaalude), opiates (e.g.,morphine), phencyclidine (PCP), propoxyphene (Darvon), and LSD. Rarely do employers test for all such substances. Instead, they typically focus on four or five and almost always include marijuana, cocaine, and amphetamines. Alcohol is not screened by these tests and few employers test for its use. Blood is rarely used for drug tests because it can reveal only *current* intoxication. Drugs are not present in an individual's blood once the body has recovered from their ingestion. Urine, on the other hand, will reveal drug use for very long periods.

The actual administration of the drug test is done in a controlled situation where the applicant or employee can be watched or listened to while urinating. A photo identification must be presented to verify that the individual taking the test is who she or he claims to be. To guard against possible adulteration of the urine (many methods exist to confound urine tests), they must be conducted in such a way to eliminate the possibility of adding something to the sample, substituting another person's urine, or substituting a sample obtained during a drug-free period. Elaborate preparations and precautions are required. To prevent the applicant from concealing test-confounding substances under the fingernails, for example, the administrator of the test must witness the applicant thoroughly wash the hands. "Unnecessary" garments that might conceal things must be removed. A number of forms must be filled out to verify the chain of custody of the urine sample as it finds its way through the testing process. Both the subject of the test and the person monitoring it must fill out forms indicating that the test was, in fact, done at that time and place. The urine sample, itself, must be measured for temperature at the time of collection (to prevent the substitution of another person's urine). The sample is inspected also for color (to prevent the use of water). The urine must be kept in sight of both individuals throughout the entire process of preparing it for transmittal to the lab. The federal government has published a list of 28 specific safeguards that must be taken in the actual *collection* of a urine sample. Specifications for the entire drug-test ritual require over 25 pages (Department of Health and Human Services, 1988)

There are two methods to detect drug use by examining a person's urine; immunological or chemical. The chemical method is the more accurate and relies on an examination of the molecular structure of substances in the urine. Every drug has a unique chemical structure, or "fingerprint." By comparing the molecular structure of substances in the urine to the known chemical structure of drugs, it is possible to identify reliably the presence of illegal drugs. The actual laboratory procedures required to accomplish this are elaborate and expensive. Typically the suspected drug is converted into its gaseous form and pushed through a long glass column with helium gas (the technique is known as gas chromatography). The time it takes to traverse the entire column and exit out the far end is very specific for each drug. The gas chromatograph quantifies that interval and compares it to known values for particular drugs. And as the drug exits, it is bombarded by electrons that break up the drug, and these pieces are then analyzed by a device known as a mass spectrometer. A drug will always break up into the same parts, and the mass spectrometer will determine the weights and relative amounts of each (gas chromatography/mass spectrometry is the actual technique used).

Much less expensive and less reliable is the immunological approach to drug testing. Since the body produces unique antibodies to every drug (antigen), it is possible to test for the presence of the drug by mixing an amount of antibody with the urine that might contain it. The manufacturer of the test provides a solution of drugs linked to enzymes and a solution of antibodies to those drugs obtained from animals (who have been injected with the drug). First the antibody solution is mixed with the urine. Then the solution containing the drug is added. Any drug in the urine (i.e., actual drugs excreted by the drug user) competes with the enzyme-linked drug (supplied by the manufacturer of the test) for the antibodies. When a specific drug is present in the urine, it will bind to the antibody, leaving the enzyme-linked drug that is supplied with the kit unbound to varying degrees, depending on the amount of drug in the sample. This leaves varying amounts of the enzyme-linked drug free to react with other substances in the testing solution. The degree of cloudiness in the solution that results from this reaction can be measured by a device known as a spectrophotometer. It is that reading that indicates whether a specimen is judged positive or negative for drugs (Miike, 1987).

Unfortunately, many drugs produce similar antibodies and immunological methods are not specific enough to distinguish among them. For that reason, it is possible that individuals may be tested "positive" for marijuana use because they have taken ibuprofen (Advil), positive for amphetamines because they have taken cough or diet medicines, or positive for opiates because they have ingested poppy seeds or valium (Miike, 1987:45–47; Douglas et al., 1989:12–18).

Labs that perform drug tests establish thresholds to distinguish between drug users and nonusers. A certain amount of drug must be found before the lab will determine that sample to be positive. This is because false positives (incorrectly identifying a sample as positive) are known to occur rather frequently (some tests are so sensitive that an individual could conceivably test positive for marijuana by having inhaled the secondhand smoke of someone in another room) and cutoff thresholds attempt to minimize that outcome. It is also important to note that there are no values that can indicate the level of drug required to produce intoxication. Indeed, a positive result on a drug test does not necessarily indicate any level of intoxication from the drug. . . only that some unknown amount was ingested. And since drugs are excreted at different rates by different people, two individuals who consumed vastly different quantities of the same substance may produce identical drug test results.

Immunological testing cannot identify when a person used a particular drug. Most drugs will be sufficiently eliminated from the body to be undetectable within a week or two. Marijuana is the exception, however, and can be detected for up to 11 weeks after an individual last used the drug. A positive test for drug use, therefore, tells the employer only that the person has probably used the drug at some time in the past. "Thus, urinalysis cannot tell whether a subject's drug use interferes with his job performance and cannot discriminate between off-duty drug use and intoxication on the job." Because of this, "workplace drug urinalysis can be used only to help an employer evaluate an employee's *morals, values, character, and trustworthiness*" (Douglas et al., 1989:12–19, emphasis added).

In view of the fallibility of these tests, labs recommended that employers conduct a second "confirmatory" test using chemical techniques on any sample found to be "positive" with immunological methods. Biostatisticians refer to a test's sensitivity (a test's ability to correctly identify samples containing drugs) and to its specificity (the ability to correctly identify drug-free urine samples). The most popular screening tests (enzyme multiplied immunoassay test or EMIT tests) are highly sensitive (always better than 95 percent), although not nearly as specific (only 85 percent or better). For illustration, consider a drug screening test that is 95 percent sensitive and 85 percent specific (like the EMIT test) and is applied to a population of 100 people of which 10 percent actually has drugs in their urine. When the test is applied to the 10 people who have drugs in their urine, it will correctly identify all of them (the odds of correctly identifying a user are .95) resulting in 10 positive test results. When the test is applied to the 90 individuals who do *not* have drugs in their urine, however, the 85 percent specificity means that 15 percent of these 90, or 13 of them, will also result in a positive test result. In total, the use of the test on 100 people will identify 23 (the 10 users and 13 nonusers) as positive. Therefore, less than half of the positive tests (10 of 23 or 43 percent) are, in fact, correct (Miike, 1987:37). In other words, when applied to a population in which only average percentages of people actually use drugs, half or more of the positive screening tests will be false positives as shown by confirmatory testing. Such "confirmatory" testing, however, is not universal. A U.S. Congressional committee found over a quarter of employers to rely *solely* on the results of the screening (immunological) tests (Committee on Government Operations, 1988:11).

There is very little good evidence that drug testing of applicants or employees reduces the problems at which they are directed. Indeed, even among public agencies that are required by law to conduct drug tests, there is no agency charged with *evaluating the effectiveness* of such programs. Drug testing programs lack objective goals. Therefore, it is virtually impossible to determine whether they work. If many applicants or employees are "caught," the drug testing program may be judged a success because it caught or filtered out these deviants. If the program does not catch many people, it may be judged a success because it deterred so many from using drugs. "Before we can assess the achievements of this drug testing plan, we have to have some specific goals as to what the testing plan seeks to achieve" (Sikorski, 1988).

To return to a point made earlier, drug tests cannot detect when a particular substance was ingested. Nor can they determine whether an individual was intoxicated by the substance. That is why drug testing has been described as testing morals, values, beliefs, and truthfulness—the essential components of individual reputation.

Conclusion

Historical data on drug testing are rather good, although the practice is very recent in origin. Data on the other types of ordeals discussed in this chapter are considerably more problematic. The only national historical information on employer testing is from an annual survey conducted by the Career Development and Placement Services at Michigan State University. Each year since 1971, a very large number of employers (approximately 10,000) who hire *college graduates* has been sent a lengthy survey about employment prospects and practices. Occasionally, this survey has included questions about employment testing of various sorts. Two very important limitations must be noted. First, these data reflect those employers who responded—typically fewer than a thousand. Other employers may differ from those who participated. Each year may, in fact, represent a different segment of employers. Second, the employers who are sent the questionnaire are those who are known to employ college graduates (the survey is sponsored by a university career planning and placement office). Whether such firms differ in significant ways from others who do not hire college graduates is unknown. We know, however, that certain preemployment practices (e.g., integrity tests) are aimed primarily at nonmanagerial applicants. To the extent these data err in the prevalence estimates they provide, we may assume that they underestimate—that a sample of *all* employers (including those who hire employees with fewer educational credentials) would show more testing—not less. No information is available from these surveys about the use of polygraphs (such a question was asked in only 2 years).

There are many years for which no information is available and the wording of questions was not always consistent. In some years employers were asked to report about the use of "attitude" tests, while in other years they responded about "honesty tests." And for some years, questions were asked only about "psychological tests." In some years employers were given a simple "Yes/No" response format to the questions while in others they could respond "Always" to "Never." In Figure 5 the line for "psychological tests" was drawn by using reports of *any* psychological test—honesty, attitude, or personality test required at least "Sometimes." Questions about drug testing were consistent beginning in 1984 (the first year such questions were asked).

Despite some rather wide fluctuations in the use of psychological testing, the overall trend is clear and consistent. At least since 1977, the use of such tests has increased twofold with the most pronounced changes occurring since 1980. The line for drug tests is much steeper showing a tripling between 1987 and 1990. Figures for 1991 (not plotted) indicate even more reliance on drug testing with 59 percent of employers claiming to use them. For both types of ordeals, therefore, use of them has increased (as have emancipation rates). The trends for emancipation and ordeals, of course, are only roughly parallel as we would expect. Employer screening is not directed *solely* at young people. Many other factors influence decisions about how to hire employees (especially the cost of preemployment screening and legal considerations). Still, the trends shown in the graph are consistent with the argument that ordeals are more likely to be used when other bases of reputation are unavailable.

Research on the type of firms that rely on these strategies supports such a conclusion. That research has shown that *larger firms* are much more likely to use these tests. For example, in 1990 Hayge estimated that 46 percent of larger firms (those employing 250 or more people) had drug testing programs compared with only 3 percent of firms that employed fewer than 50 people (Hayge, 1991:26). Of course the same could be said of Human Resource Managers—larger firms are generally more likely to rely on an official organ within the firm to assist in employment decisions. And that makes good sense. Larger firms are presented with many more applicants for positions and must make many more decisions about hiring. Lengthy personal interviews are now described as "impractical." Consider the advice given by several advocates of integrity testing: "The costs of adequately screening personnel with traditional methods, like pre-employment interviewing, are rapidly becoming prohibitive. Com-

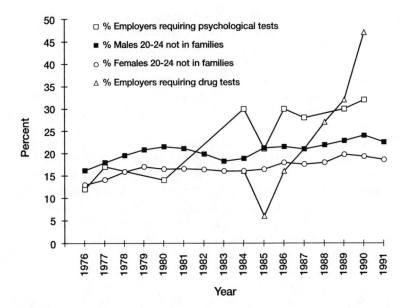

Figure 5. Trends in preemployment testing and emancipation:
1976–1990.

Source: Michigan State University, Career Development and Placement Services. 1991. *Recruiting Trends: 1990–1991,* and annual volumes for earlier years.
See Appendices A and B for figures used in all graphs.

prehensive interviewing is time consuming and often impractical or even unreasonable for the majority of entry-level jobs" (Werner, Joy, and Jones, 1991:55).

It is the magnitude of the task that argues for these techniques. Confronted with numerous applicants, none of whom is known to the employer, some "objective" method is needed to sort out the honest from the dishonest. Small firms may have the luxury of relying on personal referrals or lengthy "comprehensive" interviews. But such strategies are impractical for organizations of any size.

Larger firms are also much more likely to be subject to federal hiring laws that prohibit discrimination of various sorts. The employer of 50 or more cannot legally refuse to hire an applicant based on his or her race, religion, or sex. To the extent that these personal characteristics are believed to help sort the "good" from the "bad" risks, employers who are forbidden to rely on them may turn to ordeals and other screening strategies.

When presented with large numbers of strangers to choose from, employers must resolve the intolerable uncertainties associated with such choices. In the absence of an "old boy" network or some equivalent form of referral (i.e., in the absence of evidence of a good reputation) there is no way for humans to know which among them is to be trusted. As noted, credentials may resolve some of the uncertainty, but certainly not all. Recourse to ordeals such as the polygraph, integrity test, or tests of body fluids is a response to this uncertainty. Such ordeals may establish or sustain good reputations.

Several years ago a very bright student of mine was interviewed for a position with an international bank. As part of her final interview she was required to take a drug test. I asked her whether this was troubling and she replied "No, I don't use drugs." She saw absolutely nothing strange or untoward in such a requirement for a job. Indeed, surveys show that most Americans share that view. In a *New York Times*/CBS poll in 1986, three-fourths of full-time employees were willing to take a drug test and did not see it as an unfair invasion of their privacy. Other national surveys reveal similar levels of support for the practice (see J. Michael Walsh and Jeanne Trumble, "The Politics of Drug Testing," chapter 2 in Coombs and West, 1991). Ordeals of this sort have become routine and acceptable strategies for resolving otherwise unanswerable questions. They are not generally seen as "invasions of privacy." Instead they are accepted as one of the costs of privacy. It was certainly not privacy (as we now use that word) that made reputations obscure and led to the use of ordeals in the Middle Ages. But it was then, as it is now, those who lack reputations who were the subjects of ordeals.

5

CONCLUSION

Introduction

I have described significant changes this century in the amount of personal privacy Americans enjoy and in the number of strangers in their everyday lives. But there is no implication drawn that such changes make us "worse" in any significant way. Rather, my point is that modern times resemble closely days gone by in many essential respects. Most importantly, individual reputation continues to guide social life and commerce. What has changed is how our reputations are established and maintained. One of the most obvious consequences of our greater privacy is the difficulty in establishing and maintaining reputations. I have argued that surveillance is the way our society manages the reputations of strangers.

Earlier I made the point that reputations are always rather sketchy. Our impressions of one another are incomplete accounts of deeds and values. Impressions are based on what is, or may be, known about another person. After all, a credential tells us something about another person, but not that much. Likewise, ordeals may establish minimal claims to conformity, but only minimal claims. A very great deal of information is left unknown. But one of the messages of this chapter is that more and more *is believed to be knowable*. Indeed, one might imagine a time in the future when surveillance is so effective that it would be possible to establish objectively the most minute and intimate facts about others—to establish much more detailed and extensive reputations. Such a time might be one of the utmost personal privacy. If privacy was so pervasive that the only things known about others were those things established by credentials and ordeals, what would reputations consist of? What would be known? Answering this question amounts, I believe, to imagining a future that is the extreme version of what is actually very likely. There is no indication that the forces producing privacy (and strangers) are likely to be reversed any time soon.

To answer this question, we must first ask "What is not now known?" Private things, it should be remembered, are those that are defined as legitimately beyond scrutiny. All realms of privacy, by definition, are immune to monitoring. Living arrangements and the activities that take place in the home are (at least for the past 25 years) conspicuous examples. Privacy grows as more and more realms of our lives are defined to be beyond others' legitimate knowledge. Alternatively, privacy grows by defining ever more categories of others as removed from our personal lives. The actual limits of privacy are defined by the unknowable requirements for social solidarity. There is probably some point at which additional amounts of personal privacy make communities or organizations unworkable. However, that limit would be reached *only* when trust is no longer possible. It is, after all, trust that sustains group solidarity. And it is others' reputations that permit us to trust them. So long as we are able to trust others, privacy can expand. The limits to privacy are the limits of trust.

When we turn our attention to those areas of our lives where trust is essential, it is clear that trust permits people to enter into risky relationships. We really do not need to trust those with whom we share no relationship nor those with whom our relationships are totally free of risks. Trust may counter the insecurities produced by potential losses or injuries from a relationship. Surveillance, therefore, is a response to risks. The greater the imagined or potential losses from relationships of particular types, the greater will be the surveillance over one or both parties to them.

The type of risks countered by surveillance, however, are those inherent in relationships with strangers. Virtually any relationship may embody elements of potential harm. But relationships with strangers are the ones made easier by credentials and ordeals. As I have documented in earlier chapters, the twentieth century has been witness to growing numbers and varieties of strangers.

Following tradition, and for convenience, let us define human relationships as occurring in five basic institutional areas: the family, religion, education, the economy, and the state. The first two are the intimate institutions. Although it is true that changing family structures, divorces, and remarriages may introduce new members into existing intimate networks, such people (e.g., stepparents) are part of the family members' private lives. They are not strangers as I have used that term in this book. Inadequate though they may initially be, new adult family members' reputations *are* known. Similarly, relationships that are part of the religious institutions are typically governed by some form of membership ritual. "Joining a church" still requires some type of examination or oath. Members know one another, at a minimum, through such rituals. Reputations, though sketchy, are known. In neither family nor religion does one often find it necessary to trust strangers (defined as those without known reputations).

On the other hand, relationships in the institutions of education, the economy, and the state (if such relationships exist) are much more likely to involve strangers. In these institutional areas, relationships are more likely to be purely instrumental, directed toward the accomplishment or acquisition of some specified outcome that defines the risk. In the economy, for example, the relationship between creditor and borrower exposes the creditor to the risk of default. So too, as discussed earlier in this book, the relationship between employer and employee exposes the employer to the risk of financial loss. Legal liability may also enter into calculations of risk. Workers may sue their employers for various consequences of working in a workplace (exposure to toxic substances, for example). The insurance underwriter must tolerate risks based on life expectancies and health behavior. Life-styles are central to the calculation of medical risks. In education, selective admission policies of private secondary schools or of colleges and universities expose those institutions to the risk of student failure if unwise selections are made. In public schools, administrators risk political and financial support should large numbers of students fail. In the realm of relationships with the state, voters are asked to trust their elected officials to represent their interests. The risks involved in such relationships are varied depending on the particular individual, but may be tangible (e.g., the loss of governmental contracts) or intangible (e.g., alienation). Likewise, citizens are asked to trust the judgments of the judiciary in matters that significantly affect their personal lives. Courts must contemplate the risks to others as a result of the sentences meted out to those convicted of crimes. It is in these institutions, or, more correctly, over individuals involved in such relationships, that we should expect the greatest future increases in surveillance. Although it may not be possible to anticipate the types of credentials and ordeals that may become commonplace in the future, there are certain trends that already suggest future directions.

What will people want to know about others before they will enter into risky relationships with them in a future of vastly expanded privacy? As they always have, reputations will establish that the parties to a relationship may be trusted. This will not change. Rather, the *method* used to obtain such information and the *quantity* of such information will both change. Most importantly, however, reputation will become more *prospective*; it will predict the future as well as reflect the past.

Reputations, of course, have always been viewed as predictive. In fact, there is hardly any other reason to be concerned with them. Before entering into any risky relationship with another person, I want to know as much as I can about him to permit me to *predict* the consequences of our alliance. However, such predictions have always been inferred. The well-known scoundrel is *unlikely* to change. The trusted colleague is *unlikely* to become a traitor. The job applicant who tests positive for cocaine usage or "fails" an integrity test is *unlikely* to be a good risk. The M.BA. from Wharton is *probably* very capable of becoming an excellent manager. But as I have shown throughout this book, existing ordeals and credentials are not terribly accurate. They all err in both directions— establishing as untrustworthy those who probably are and establishing as trustworthy those who probably are not. No existing form of surveillance establishes a reliable link between the information obtained (in credentials or ordeals) and future behaviors. The trends I describe in this chapter relate to methods by which future behaviors *are linked, scientifically*, to background information about an individual.

In the following sections I consider changes in the workplace, schools, and the legal system (economy, education, and state) that pertain to how reputations are established. These trends are united in their reliance on scientific methods for characterizing individuals. Scientific advances are making it easier and easier to know more and more things about people. And as such information becomes increasingly available, it appears to be increasingly demanded by the public institutions. This is especially true of predictive (prospective) information.

Genetic and Biochemical Reputations

The "new" information that is available about people is contained in the molecular or chemical structure of their body, or in their genes. Genetic science has advanced to a point where it is now possible to "diagnose" at least 350 genetic diseases by examining a minute sample of tissue (blood, hair, semen, etc.) (U.S. Congress, Office of Technology Assessment, 1990b: Chapter 5). Various imaging techniques now permit us to visualize the interior structure of the brain or other internal organs. Sophisticated nuclear and magnetic analyses permit us to study the actual processing of information by the brain.

The way all such procedures work is by establishing a statistical definition of "normal," which becomes a standard against which to measure individual differences. When an individual's genetic, chemical, or morphological profile differs from "normal" that person is "diagnosed" as ill, deviant, or abnormal. And as the arsenal of tests expands, there will necessarily be more individuals who are defined as *not* normal. This is absolutely unavoidable. Whatever is being tested will have a known distribution. The vast majority of those tested will fall in the "normal" range, but a certain percentage, by definition, will always be outside that range. Without a test, those "abnormal" individuals could not be labeled that way (though other information might lead to the same reputation).

Conformity to *statistical* norms may not immediately appear to resemble the type of conformity ascertained by more traditional methods of surveillance. Indeed, individual reputations have heretofore reflected conformity to *moral* norms. A person with a good name was one who was known to abide by the important rules. But ideas about conformity are changing. In particular, ideas about *why* people do or do not conform are changing. Behavior is increasingly coming to be viewed as a product of body chemistry, brain structure, and genetic inheritance rather than moral probity, self-restraint, or social conditions. If it is believed that behavior can be linked to something objectively knowable about the body, it follows that one can isolate the *causes* of deviance (or conformity). It becomes possible to explain both past actions *and* to predict future ones *scientifically*. Reputation thereby becomes (or appears to become) scientifically predictive of future behaviors.

Genetic tests are used in both prenatal screening and in the identification of adults whose genes display abnormalities (see Nelkin and Tancredi, 1989). Amniocentesis and chorionic villus sampling, for example, are both strategies for extracting tissue from a pregnant woman to permit various tests of the fetus's DNA. These tests are capable of identifying up to 180 genetic disorders. Physicians also perform genetic tests on individuals who are thinking about starting a family. Such tests identify diseases and disorders that can be passed along to offspring. To date, most identifiable disorders are products of a single gene disorder. A few examples include Huntington's disease, sickle-cell anemia, cystic fibrosis, hemophilia, adult polycystic kidney disease, retinoblastoma, and phenylketonuria. However, genetic research on problems caused or linked to multiple-gene disorders has identified groups of genes that appear to cause some forms of (among other illnesses) cancer, emphysema, juvenile diabetes, Alzheimer's disease, cleft palate, heart disease, atherosclerosis, and mental illness (Nelkin and Tancredi, 1989:28).

The Human Genome Project is an international effort to map the entire human genome. When completed early next century, the entire set of genes that comprise human DNA will be known and mapped. That map will permit scientists to identify the genetic disorders that are associated with nearly all 3,000 known genetic diseases.

In addition to genetic mapping, recent advances in neurochemical research have identified many of the neurotransmitters that drive brain functions. The relationship between the presence of various brain chemicals and psychological or mental states is the major focus of such research.

Such efforts have been dramatically advanced by recent developments in imaging technology. The older methodologies (computer assisted tomography, or CAT scans, and magnetic resonance imaging, or MRI) allowed researchers to visualize human tissues. But positron emission tomography (PET) allows researchers to actually "watch" the brain function. An individual is given an injection of a substance containing positron-emitting isotopes. When this radioactive material decays, by-products are recorded by detectors and a computer assembles the information on a visual display. Brain function can then be watched in response to stimuli or particular behaviors. Even more sophisticated, superconducting quantum interference devices (SQUIDs) use magnetic sensors to detect fields produced in the brain. So sophisticated is the SQUID it is possible to visualize neurons to detect which parts of the brain are operating under different conditions. Research currently under way on high-energy electron imaging allows visualization of *subcellular* (structures *within* a cell) particles.

> We are approaching a time when imaging techniques will be able to "see" how persons respond to sights and sounds, how muscles provide feedback for motor coordination, and how people pay attention. They will be able to monitor biologically the state of the brain when it is affected by sleep, drugs, nutrition, or the stimulation of ideas. And like the genetic tests, imaging techniques can be used not only to detect the actual presence of disease in a population but to predicting who may be predisposed to becoming ill at some future time. (Nelkin and Tancredi, 1989:32)

The scientific basis for all these various tests gives each of them the appearance of true objectivity. When it is found that certain structural or chemical patterns are correlated with behavioral or mental patterns, it is only a short leap to concluding that one is the cause of the other. Just as the lie detector test or paper and pencil integrity test is ordinarily given greater weight than the reports of individuals about their honesty, so genetic or other types of screening tests are usually given greater credence than other kinds of information about the people being tested. It is well known, for example, that individual characteristics such as height, weight, intelligence, or (increasingly) personality have both a genetic and an environmental component. But with the increasing sophistication of genetic testing, the temptation is to interpret all conditions known to have a genetic component as if genetics were the sole determining influence. As Nelkin and Trancredi (1989) note, this tendency is understandable because research on single-gene defects such as Huntington's disease has linked the genetic defect *unambiguously* with the symptoms of the disease.

However, most traits are the product of numerous genes *and* the interaction of them with a person's environment. The presence of a particular genetic pattern *may* eventually produce certain behaviors or illnesses. But it may not. For example, phenylketonuria (PKU) is an inherited disease that produces mental retardation in an individual *if* that person consumes phenylalanine. A diet free of phenylalanine will prevent the appearance of the symptoms of the disease.

When applied to various mental states or illnesses, genetic predictions are especially susceptible to error. It may be, for example, that identifiable genetic abnormalities on chromosome 11 are associated with manic depression. Research has found that between 60 and 70 percent of those with this abnormality become mentally ill. But, of course, 30 to 40 percent do not. What is true for *populations of individuals* has little relevance to *specific individuals*. Predictions of future problems that are based on statistical relationships of this sort are not relevant to specific *individuals* although they are certainly relevant to entire populations. But genetic tests *are* applied to individuals. And once a genetic abnormality is discovered, clinicians classify all those with it as alike. The scientific basis of these tests makes them appear to be more reliable than other sorts of information that might also be available about people. False diagnoses (labeling an individual who manifests a genetic abnormality as ill or potentially ill when they are not) have tremendous consequences for particular individuals so identified. To be falsely diagnosed as having a predisposition to schizophrenia, for example, will probably lead to numerous instances of discrimination. For the individual, the consequences of error are potentially drastic.

For the institution doing the testing, however, the consequences of relying on less-than-perfect screening tests are not very large at all. The employer who uses genetic screens of applicants risks very little as a result of using an imperfect "test." Indeed, from the organizational perspective, such imperfect tests are undoubtedly viewed as a significant boon (Nelkin and Tancredi, 1989:47). By being able to predict the future health and/or functioning of a proportion of individuals, public institutions reduce costs and improve efficiency. Health and life insurers may screen out those with potentially debilitating or costly future illnesses. Employers, likewise, may screen out the health risks as well as those likely to develop specific mental illnesses. Individuals may be screened to determine whether they are susceptible to problems caused by workplace environmental conditions (various chemicals, for example). Schools may relegate to "special education" those children with biochemical patterns suggestive of "hyperactivity" or "attention deficit disorder." In all cases, such organizational strategies work to the advantage of the organization. They do this, however, at great cost to those incorrectly identified as "abnormal." And there will always be some who are incorrectly identified.

The Workplace

Though not yet widespread, U.S. employers are now subjecting workers to genetic tests. Several large chemical firms began genetic testing in the 1970s in an attempt to identify and exclude those predisposed to illness when exposed to certain chemicals. With the growing acceptance (by both employers and job applicants) of testing body tissue, genetic screening for employment has also grown in acceptability. Such screening is now done as a part of a *medical* examination. The rationale for such testing, in fact, is often made on medical grounds (e.g., to exclude job applicants who are likely to develop illnesses as a result of exposure to workplace hazards, or to reduce the costs of medical insurance). The new medical dimension to DNA testing, however, is that such tests may predate the onset of symptoms by many years. Heathy individuals at high or low risk of developing a disease at some time in the future may be identified. Traditionally, medical tests have been conducted to diagnose existing conditions (see Huggins et al., 1990).

Two types of workplace genetic tests are possible. *Genetic monitoring* refers to periodically examining employees to evaluate changes of their genetic material (e.g., chromosomal damage or evidence of increased occurrence of molecular mutations) that might have evolved in the course of employment. The presumed cause is workplace exposure to hazardous substances. The premise is that such changes could indicate increased risk of future illness. (U.S. Congress, Office of Technology Assessment, 1990b:4) *Genetic screening* refers to examination of the genetic makeup of either employees or job applicants for certain *inherited* characteristics. Screening, in other words, differs from monitoring in that screening searches for *preexisting* genetic conditions, monitoring searches for *changes* in genetic materials.

Workplace genetic screening may be done to determine whether an employee or applicant has an inherited predisposition or susceptibility to illnesses should the person be exposed to certain workplace conditions. Alternatively, employees or job applicants could be screened to detect conditions not associated with the workplace in any way. Whereas monitoring focuses on hazardous *workplace conditions* that might cause changes, screening is a one-time test that looks for inherited conditions that workers bring with them to the job and that are beyond their control.

There are many possible motives for genetic testing by an employer. These procedures are applied to people who show no outward signs of illness. In this sense, they resemble drug tests. Employers who resort to either are concerned that what they otherwise know about an individual is not sufficient. The costs of hiring, promoting, or retaining an employee may be reduced if the employer is able to anticipate correctly conditions that lead to lower productivity. This is especially true for employers who are concerned about health insurance costs. By identifying "carriers" of predisposing genetic abnormalities, employers may be able to forego the costs involved in caring for such employees. Unfortunately, the ability to *identify and diagnose* genetic problems has advanced much faster than has the corresponding potential for *treating* those with such problems. As such, the alternatives available to the employer who uses genetic testing are quite limited. Once a problem is diagnosed, little can be done except to *exclude* that person from the workplace or from particular locations in it.

The biggest problem with all such genetic tests is that they cannot factor environmental risks into their diagnoses. In monitoring efforts, for example, it is assumed that *if* damage to genetic material is discovered, this represents the first stage in a process that may lead to illness. However, as noted by the U.S. Congress, Office of Technology Assessment (1990b:9), "The connections between chromosomal damage and disease are unclear except in a small number of cancer cases. Most analysts agree that interpretation of [genetic test] results at the individual level is questionable and recommend that until the relationship between [genetic] damage and disease is better understood, interpretation should be limited to the population level." And with respect to genetic screening for such inherited predispositions to such things as heart disease, hardening of the arteries, cancer, mental illness, or diabetes, the environment plays an equally unknown but vital role. "The influence of the environment . . . remains the wild card in most cases, because possession of the genetic predisposition alone may be insufficient to cause disease. It is likely that for some time modern science will be more successful in identifying the genes and the markers than in identifying the environmental agent(s) necessary for activation of the predisposing genes (U.S. Congress, Office of Technology Assessment, 1990b:11).

The Americans with Disabilities Act passed in 1990 (PL 101–336) prohibits discrimination in employment on the basis of disabilities. The law forbids both public and private employers from discriminating against people with disabilities in hiring, firing, pay, or conditions of work if the disability does not interfere with the person's ability to function on the job. Further, the law prohibits the administration of medical tests as a part of preemployment considerations unless the testing would provide information about the person's ability to perform on the job. This would appear to prohibit genetic screening for conditions that are not specifically related to performance of the job. However, there is no specific language in the law pertaining to genetic monitoring or screening (U.S. Congress, Office of Technology Assessment, 1990b:114–116).

As I noted at the outset, genetic testing is not yet widespread, In fact, the practice is quite rare. The Office of Technology Assessment surveyed the 500 largest employers (Fortune 500) , the 50 largest utilities, and 33 major labor unions in 1989. The purpose of the survey was to determine the extent of genetic testing in the workplace. Only 5 percent of surveyed firms used genetic screening or monitoring in 1989. Another 2 percent of companies reported that they anticipated using such tests in the next 5 years. And 40 percent reported that they were "Not Sure" (U.S. Congress, Office of Technology Assessment, 1990b:22–24).

The Human Genome Project will have mapped all 50,000 to 150,000 human genes within the next two decades. With the template for the entire human genetic makeup as background, individual DNA profiles will be immensely more informative. The extent to which employers will use such information will depend on the costs and the legal requirements associated with it—not solely on the predictive value. Even if restricted to using *only* job-related medical tests (i.e., if restricted to testing only for genetic signs of job-related disabilities) there is nothing to prevent employers from conducting full genetic screens once they possess the tissue sample. As noted by the American Medical Association's Office of General Counsel, this is a very possible and likely event. "If an employer could perform tests that were not job related and were to use the information in making employment decisions, it would be difficult for an individual to prove that the test results influenced a particular decision. The employer could simply claim that other factors led to the outcome that occurred." (American Medical Association, 1990:1005).

Genetic material is the basis for many human traits. To the extent that it becomes possible to establish clear and reliable links between behavioral patterns or diseases and individual genetic makeup, there is little reason to suspect that such information will not be used. Once the human genome is mapped, it will be possible to describe every individual by his or her unique genetic composition. Data banks that now contain information about individuals' marital status, credit ratings, insurance records, or health information could easily be expanded to include a complete record of their genetic makeup. "Some biotechnology firms are predicting that most people will have their genetic profile on record by the year 2000" (Nelkin and Trancredi, 1989:159). Compared with the amount of information now available in credential files, genetic profiles will afford vastly more. And that information will be much better for the purposes of identifying individuals or predicting their future health and/or behavior.

A genetic profile of an individual stored in a computer or encoded on a magnetic strip on a card will amount to a complete body and brain scan.

The link between behaviors and genetic patterns is still rather weak. However, the link between *biochemistry* and behavior seems somewhat stronger. Indeed, the chemical bases of numerous behavioral patterns is increasingly accepted. Attempts to alter behaviors deemed undesirable are often made by administering drugs that alter the biochemical imbalance. The reliance on chemistry to explain and modify behavior is nowhere more apparent than in our public schools.

Schools

American public schools have always been charged with solving conspicuous social problems. The assimilation of foreigners, racial integration, or solving inadequate international economic competitiveness are a few of the problems Americans have asked their schools to tackle. In their dual roles as educators and social reformers, schools have struggled to implement educational theories (or philosophies) that appeared to accomplish their objectives while also satisfying parents, local school boards, and those political bodies that provide funding. As noted earlier, American schools have traditionally relied on testing to sort out the winners from the losers, the bright from the not so bright, the capable from the incapable. To do this, educators have traditionally relied on testing. The emphasis on testing has not recently changed so much as the type of testing that is done.

Testing has been, and remains, a very prominent feature of public schools. Standardized tests, in particular, figure quite importantly in the administration of our public education system. Such tests have been used to structure curricular programs to accomplish both educational and political goals. The big change in recent years, however, has been the increasing focus on *biological* bases of student performance.

At least since the 1920s, intelligence has been viewed as a measurable trait that could explain student performance and provide a basis for matching a student (i.e., tracking) with an "appropriate" curriculum. An IQ score was viewed for many years as a measure of ability. By the middle 1960s, however, IQ tests were increasingly challenged as "culturally biased." Certain categories of students appeared routinely to score lower on standardized intelligence tests. This fueled a debate over whether intelligence was inherited (i.e., a product of genetics) or a product of social conditions (especially socioeconomic conditions). At the turn of the twentieth century, intelligence (as measured by an IQ test) was viewed almost unquestionably as being immutable and inherited. By the 1970s, however, most school psychologists described IQ scores as reflecting *both* genetics and social environments. Still, however, intelligence as a trait is believed to be measurable *and* inherited (despite debates over *how much* is inherited and how much is environmental). Since intelligence *is* (by most educators and professionals) accepted as a legitimate mental trait, the problems in group performance on IQ tests came to be seen as problems in the *tests*, themselves.

> By the 1970s standardized tests began to reflect the emerging scientific metaphors of the brain. No longer seen as a single entity, intelligence came to be defined in terms of neurological circuitry and was assumed to include many separate functions. An assignment of IQ is no longer considered sufficient to classify a child. Thus tests today include psychological indicators, and school records contain extensive psychological information about individuals and their families . . . The range of tests that children were exposed to in the 1970s . . . [covered] not only the familiar categories (learning disabled, minimal brain damaged, emotionally handicapped, visually handicapped) but also include scales rating children for impulse control, intellectuality, withdrawal and social behavior." (Nelkin and Tancredi, 1989:115)

Students who have trouble learning or who misbehave in the classroom are now described by reference to biochemical imbalances. For example, young boys who are disruptive, aggressive, and inattentive in class are often "diagnosed" as being hyperactive (more recently called *attention deficit disorder*). The brains of such children (90 percent of whom are boys), it is now believed, process information more slowly than normal. This makes it difficult for such children to understand materials presented in the classroom. Unable to make sense of what is going on, such children become bored and restless. Once this theory was accepted, the solution was found in chemical stimulants of brain activity. A stimulant, it was believed, would speed up the processing of information by the brain, thereby allowing a child to understand the materials presented at a normal pace. The use of the drug Ritalin (a neurological stimulant) does, in fact, appear to calm restless students although there is little evidence that it improves learning or lengthens attention spans. Nonetheless, since the chemical stimulant often resolves the most immediate problem (behavioral problems in the classroom) many educators now believe that the theory attributing attention deficit disorder to brain functioning is supported (Nelkin and Tancredi, 1989:119–121).

Reading problems, similarly, are now often attributed to brain dysfunctions. Students who have difficulty reading have been examined with sophisticated brain imaging devices. Such research has led to the development of a theory linking such problems with particular abnormalities in the cerebral cortex of the brain. The disorder, now known as dyslexia, is believed by some to be of genetic origin (National Institute of Mental Health, 1989).

Together, scientific advances in genetic and imaging technologies and a willingness to envision behavior as rooted in body chemistry or genes promise to help educators identify those students who will have problems in school—to *predict* future behaviors. Genes and chemicals, if viewed as the *cause* of behaviors or learning, allow educators and scientists to make predictions about how individuals will fare in school. Appropriate interventions therefore come to be seen as *medical*— (e.g., altering brain chemistry) rather than social/environmental (e.g., altering the structure of the classroom). Problems with learning, therefore, are increasingly attributed to chemical or structural disorders of the brain. In 1979, only 29 percent of all handicapped students were diagnosed as "learning disabled." In 1988 that percentage was 47 percent (U.S. Statistical Abstract, 1990: Table 239).

To what extent is a student's measured *ability* to learn (as determined by tests or medical diagnoses) a part of his or her educational credentials? Actually, a diagnosis of being learning disabled may figure into a student's academic record, but there is not, as yet, any way for such information to be available outside the school context. Suppose, however, that we continue to pursue the links between learning and physiology (which we surely will). And suppose we are able to establish clear connections between them (which, some believe, we may). Then biochemical and genetic profiles may become even *more* significant than other academic records. After all, academic records (today's educational credentials) reflect only past accomplishments. Whether they are accurate predictors of future accomplishments or failures is, as many employers realize, problematic. But if *science* can provide a prospective credential that is widely believed to be reliable and valid, will this not become more desirable than school records that are such imperfect predictors of future potentials?

Courts of Law

Thus far I have described trends in employment and schooling that elevate the biological bases of behavior to ever greater prominence. The same trends already described may also be seen in our public courts of law.

Genetic or biochemical information about individuals figures into legal decisions in several ways. First, medical opinions are accepted to help the

Court determine whether the accused is culpable. In sentencing, medical evaluations are often used to assess the potential danger of releasing a defendant back into the public as well as the likelihood of rehabilitation. In assembling evidence, genetic "fingerprints" are increasingly used to identify and convict suspects.

If a criminal act can be shown to be the result of a medical condition rather than intention, then the action may be deemed not criminal. As Nelkin and Trancredi note in their book *Dangerous Diagnoses* (1989), courts and lawyers are increasingly willing to define criminal acts as medical problems. To support this claim, the authors describe several widely publicized trials in the past 15 years. In 1979, a policeman who shot a 15-year-old boy was found not guilty because he had a psychosis associated with epilepsy. The Court and jury accepted the claim of an association between temporal lobe seizures (a symptom of epilepsy) and uncontrolled violence. In 1985, a Florida man was acquitted of murder because he was diagnosed as having suffered brain damage caused by solvent fumes and drug use. After John Hinkley shot President Reagan in 1982, he was found not guilty by reason of insanity. While the prosecution introduced expert witness opinions that Hinckley was sane, the defense offered *biological* evidence that he was not. A brain scan showed that the defendant's brain had "shrunk."

Other applications of medical science in courts of law include the use of tissue typing to establish paternity, or brain scans to identify problems that make it unlikely that a defendant can be rehabilitated. Most recently, genetic "fingerprinting" has become a very highly publicized legal strategy.

Since every human has a unique genetic makeup, a profile of any person's DNA will unambiguously distinguish that person from any other. DNA is found in all human cells except red blood cells (although other cells found in blood do contain DNA). If it is possible to obtain a sample of tissue, blood, or semen from a crime site, the DNA contained in such a sample can be used to identify the individual who left it. In rape cases, for example, semen obtained from the victim may be used to produce the DNA makeup of the rapist. When a suspect is then accused of the crime, his DNA can be compared with that left at the scene of the crime. If it matches, there is virtually no chance that the individual was not the perpetrator. If it does not match, by the same token, there is virtually no chance that the individual was the perpetrator.

The use of DNA to identify individuals has received widespread approval by scientists. The U.S. Congress, Office of Technology Assessment (1990b) endorses the practice when it is done properly. The first use of DNA testing in a court of law was in 1986 and forensic DNA analysis has since been admitted into evidence in at least 185 cases by 38 States and the

U.S. military (as of January 1, 1990) (U.S. Congress, Office of Technology Assessment, 1990b:14). Such tests are much more widely used in investigation than in the prosecution of cases. As such, DNA testing is more widespread than its judicial use might suggest.

Fingerprints are now stored in digitized computer files. Law enforcement officials may connect to centralized databanks to determine whether or not a print found at a crime scene or obtained from a suspect matches a criminal record stored in a central computer file at the FBI. The U.S. Congress, Office of Technology Assessment (1990b:19) endorses the idea of adding DNA profiles to such databanks: "Centralized or linked databases containing DNA profiles would permit rapid, electronic comparison of results from tests on different samples within a laboratory and among laboratories nationwide." But this same agency notes that there may be concerns over such a centralized databank of individual DNA profiles.

> The pervasive use of computer systems to collect personal information raises civil liberties issues and informational privacy concerns. Social security numbers are personal, as are fingerprints. Use or misuse of personal information collected in electronic databases can affect an individual's ability to obtain employment, credit, insurance, security clearances, and other services and benefits. Not surprisingly, then, proposals to store a person's genetic information in a national network evoke several concerns about privacy. (U.S. Congress, Office of Technology Assessment, 1990b:21).

As the Office of Technology Assessment report notes, Government and private agencies regularly collect and store personal information. The real question, from the perspective of this government agency, is not whether genetic profiles should be stored, but rather how to safeguard the uses of such information. As noted in the report, many object to the routine storage of individual genetic profiles because such information can be used for many purposes *other* than identifying a culprit of a crime. However, there appears to be little obstacle to establishing a national databank of DNA profiles—at least of those convicted of crimes. How that information will be used, however, and who may have access to it are still matters to be determined.

As in the other institutional areas already discussed, there is no reason to suspect that when forensic uses of genetic material are established and verified, they will not be used. Though largely limited to identification purposes at this time, courts are increasingly willing to admit "medical" evidence linking genetic and/or biochemical makeup with criminal actions or the possibility of future rehabilitation.

Conclusion

I began this book with these questions: How, in an anonymous society of strangers, is trust possible? How is it possible to depend on or believe in other people when we do not know them or have never met them? My answer to these questions focused on the role of individual reputations. I argued that reputation is the basis for trust. Privacy, however, makes it difficult to know others' reputations. And a society of strangers is also a society with vast amounts of privacy. Trust is possible, therefore, only to the extent that reputations can be established and maintained among strangers. Before we are willing to enter into a risky relationship with another person, we desire some assurance that the other person may be trusted. Surveillance, in the form of ordeals and credentials, establishes and maintains individual reputations.

I have attempted to show how ordeals and credentials operate in our society. By using individuals who do not live in families (i.e., the *emancipated*) as an example of strangers, I showed that many types of ordeals and credentials arose and were increasingly used as the numbers of such strangers increased in our society.

Traditional forms of surveillance reviewed in this book suffer by being tied only indirectly to an individual's background or, more importantly, their future. To know that a person has passed a drug test tells us only a very little about that person's past and even less about his or her future. Similarly, to know that a person is a college graduate is to know only the most minimal things about them.

Surveillance in the future is less likely to suffer from such limitations. Indeed, to the extent that scientists are able to link behaviors and mental states to genetic and/or biochemical makeup, it will be possible to make predictions about how people are likely to act and think as well as to explain why they think or act as they do. But it will never be possible to explain or predict perfectly. No matter how sophisticated our genetic testing or imaging becomes, the "wild card" will always be the physical and social environment. How effective we will be at using environmental factors to predict and explain behaviors depends on how effective the social sciences are in their theories of human behavior, and how effectively such theories can be combined with genetic and neurochemical explanations. At this time, the social sciences are rather imprecise in many of their predictions and explanations. However, they are getting better. But social scientific explanations refer to *populations* more than to individuals. It is virtually impossible to use existing theories of behavior to predict specific outcomes for a particular individual.

Ultimately, reputations are most important in their ability to help people reduce uncertainty. The better able we are to predict and explain human behavior at the individual level, the less risk will be involved in human relationships among strangers. Paradoxically, a society full of strangers may permit more trust than one with fewer strangers. Whether it does depends on how much we can know about each other and how reliably predictive such knowledge is. But it also depends on how much we are willing to give up for our privacy.

There are many justifiable concerns that these new surveillance techniques should evoke. The application of population-based models to individuals raises the possibility of sophisticated forms of discrimination. One can imagine that genetic makeup could make it impossible for a person to obtain employment or higher education despite any real threat to the employer or educational institution. The consequences of being incorrectly "diagnosed" or labelled defective could be devastating for any person. This is but one reason to be concerned about developments in surveillance technology. There are others.

Each of the new forms of surveillance that I have discussed poses the potential for many types of abuse or misuse. Elaborate and sophisticated methods of surveillance can be used to violate privacy. Personal information can be surreptitiously obtained. These techniques can be used illegitimately to advance the interests of unscrupulous employers, investigators (public and private), retailers, marketing firms, or mass media. They could be used to uncover damaging information to blackmail (literally or figuratively) people. These are very real possibilities *but they not new ones.* The potential for abuse of privacy and individual autonomy did not arise, nor will it arise, with the development of more effective forms of surveillance. It may become easier than it once was to assemble a dossier on someone (by using a sample of their hair, for example). And that dossier may be more extensive in terms of what it implies about a person than was once possible. But currently existing forms of surveillance, as well as those of our past, could be abused in the same ways. Personal information that is presently maintained by banks, insurance companies, employers, or creditors, for example, could be disclosed without the knowledge or permission of the person who provided it.

Whether or not the new forms of surveillance are misused has less to do with the technology on which they are based than on the organizations or individuals using them. Increases in surveillance, per se do not represent abuses or invasions of privacy. It is the illegitimate use of those technologies that raises concern.

These developments in surveillance occurred in the name of widely shared and valued collective goals: freedom of the press, the protection of public order, the prevention of subversion, and administrative efficiency. They are in response to changing social conditions. In particular, they are means by which individuals who would, otherwise, be unknown may be deemed trustworthy. They arise in response to greater autonomy, anonymity, and privacy. They are the costs most people are willing to pay for their privacy.

Knowledge gained by credentials and ordeals permits the growth of privacy. And advances in surveillance technology permit ever greater amounts of privacy. But that cost of individual privacy is not inconsequential. Something is lost when privacy is gained. Surveillance may make it possible to trust people who would otherwise be total strangers, but it does not help us get to know one another. And that, as I have noted at the outset, may be the greatest cost of privacy.

The use of surveillance is likely to increase in the future. The forces that will foster a greater reliance on credentials and ordeals show no signs of abating. There is good reason to predict significant growth in the numbers of people who cannot be known except by such means. Much of this can be traced to changes in the institution of the family and the typical life course of individuals. One of the most obvious consequences of such trends as the later age at first marriage, high rates of divorce, cohabitation, and out-of-wedlock childbearing is that a growing percentage of adults is either not married or not living in families. Whereas three quarters (76 percent) of adults were married in 1965, only one in six (62 percent) were in 1989. In 1960, three quarters of American households were married couples. In 1991, slightly more than half (55 percent) were (U.S. Bureau of the Census, 1992: Table A2; U.S. Bureau of the Census, 1991a: Table N; U.S. Bureau of the Census, 1991b).

The family has served historically as the most important source of personal identity. From one's family of orientation was inherited a "family name." Likewise, to be married and, especially, to be parents has been to enjoy social (and legal) privileges associated with presumptions of maturity, responsibility, and stability.

High rates of mobility, the density of modern communities, lower rates of marriage, and the other changes in the family just noted combine to make traditional bases of reputation less important. The good family name counts little among those who do not know the family. Likewise, the unmarried person does not benefit from the minimal respect traditionally granted married people. At the same time, the need to enter into risky relationships has not diminished. In fact, it has probably increased. Americans rely increasingly on others for a wide range of services (financial, health care, transportation, education and training, recreation, and personal care). So, although many of the traditional bases of trust have declined in importance, the need to trust others in significant ways has not. Surveillance helps fill the void.

When objective and reliable information about an individual's past and likely future can be made available it will probably be used, because the lack of such information is one of the most conspicuous problems in modern complex societies. The need to trust those we do not know is an old problem. But the extent to which this type of trust is required is now greater, and possibly of greater consequence. The methods and techniques of surveillance discussed in this book address part of the problem of trusting strangers. At the same time, the ability to trust those we do not know has the potential to alter the character of public life. In our roles as employers, employees, citizens, politicians, students, teachers, borrowers or lenders, we may find it increasingly possible to interact with and trust people we do not know except by their portable reputations. Therefore, we may be able to expand our networks of associates without ever getting to know them personally.

Reliable and predictive reputations that are easily verified and widely available may subtly alter the way people interact in public. Historically, people who had earned a bad reputation had few options. They could renounce those who shamed them and claim that *their* own standards, not the other persons', were right. Or, they could accept their judgment and reform themselves to be more in line with their rules of conduct. Alternatively, individuals might relocate to a new area where they could "start over."

Portable reputations have made the last strategy less feasible. Unless someone is willing to establish an entirely new identity (which some people do), his or her past failings (e.g., bankruptcies, arrests, rejection for life insurance, occupational history) are increasingly matters of record. And newer forms of surveillance introduce another element based on *ascription*. Much of our genetic and biochemical makeup is inherited. There is no way to "escape" or alter this element of our reputations.

To the extent that such information figures into our identities, we become defined by the circumstances of our birth. Heritability of certain disabilities, for example, is specific to racial or ethnic background. Sickle-cell anemia is the most notorious example. Cystic fibrosis is also selective: it affects individuals of European descent at much higher rates than it does people of other origins (National Institutes of Health, 1990). There are undoubtedly many human disabilities and potentials that will be found to be more prevalent among certain races, ethnic groups, or members of one sex. As we discover these traits, we may be able to cure or treat them. But we may not. And if we are not able to remedy the defect, members of those groups susceptible to them are likely to face different treatment *as individuals* than are members of groups less susceptible to them. How such information could influence public life is purely a matter of speculation. However, distinctions based on ascriptive traits such as sex, race, or ethnicity (even when not based on fact) have served, historically, to justify discriminatory practices in schools, courts of law, and employment. The possibility of such discrimination is a major concern among scientists presently engaged in the Human Genome Project, although broad consensus on how to deal with such worries does not yet exist (Orentlicher, 1990).

Where it may once have been difficult for someone to escape his or her past, it may become increasingly difficult to escape one's *future* as well, at least as defined by genes and biochemistry. Once the genetic bases for Alzheimer's disease, alcoholism, diabetes, genius, or coronary artery disease are identified, for example, will schools, courts, or employers treat individuals with such genes differently? (Orentlicher, 1990). Some believe they will (Aldhous, 1991). If it becomes possible to identify a gene or a suite of genes that causes or predisposes an individual to becoming ill, employers may screen such individuals from employment or promotion. Schools may justify differential interventions to prepare young people for their likely futures. Courts may interpret such information as relevant to decisions or sentencing. Individuals may be denied immigration because of heritable diseases. Each of these possibilities is foreshadowed by practices already in place.

The nature of *intimate* life may also change as the nature of public life changes. Indeed, the use of genetic "fingerprints" to establish paternity is a conspicuous example. The relationship linking a child to an adult male has always been *social* because the biological link between them is established long before the child is born. And although different cultures handle the task of establishing paternity differently, every culture has social norms (often referred to as principles of "legitimacy") to do so. In our society, for example, the child born to a married couple is presumed (by law in many states) to be the biological offspring of the husband— regardless of actual (biological) paternity (Friedman, 1992:77). When questions of paternity arise, however, courts are turning increasingly to the use of DNA tests. These (often) irrefutable proofs of paternity promise to secure financial support for abandoned mothers and children. They promise the biological father of a child access to that child in a paternal role. But they also introduce a new element into one of the most basic human relationships.

More significantly, portable reputations may come to be viewed as acceptable or desirable in the realm of mate selection. Concern over the possibility of contracting HIV (the virus that is believed to cause AIDS) may lead some individuals to secure from their partners "proof" that they are not infected. Such proof, in the form of a test result, carries some moral weight because it may be evidence of an individual's past behaviors. What else will potential partners ask of each other? How much information about another's past and future will people seek when contemplating marriage? As with any such question, whether it pertains to mate selection or employment, the answer depends on the potential risks involved in trust. In matters of sexual relations, trust can be quite risky because of the possible consequences of contracting an illness that is untreatable and/or fatal.

The risks associated with marriage and intimate relationships *are* high. The majority of recent first marriages will probably end in divorce. And when that happens, there are both emotional and financial consequences for each spouse. Most married couples will have children. And when they do, there are significant consequences for the parents should the child be born with severe disabilities. Anything that might reduce the risks associated with marriage and parenthood, therefore, would be attractive. Indeed, fetal tests for various heritable diseases are already a matter of course for many older pregnant women. However, with the exception of tests for HIV and other sexually transmitted diseases, potential spouses do not have access to much in the way of diagnostic information about one another. And despite the risks involved, partners do not typically explore one anothers' legal and financial backgrounds. For example, even though credit histories and driving records are now widely available, few potential spouses obtain such information about their partners.

Whether this situation will change depends on two things. First, there must exist objective information about individuals that will reasonably pertain to the risks involved in marriages and other intimate relationships. At present there is not much, and we have no way of knowing whether such information will become available. Second, the voluntary reliance on such information depends on how widespread its use becomes in other areas of life. To many people, obtaining a complete credit history of someone with whom they are romantically involved would appear unseemly and inappropriate. Doing so appears to challenge the trust that is such a basic premise of romantic relationships. Should the reliance on recorded information about individuals continue to expand, however, this may change. What people come to accept as unremarkable in their public lives may influence their views of such practices in their private lives.

The trends and possibilities just sketched blur the distinction between the public and the private. I defined as private those things legitimately kept from others' scrutiny. The premise of this work is that we now enjoy vast amounts of privacy because it is both possible and permissible to guard much of our life from view. Today's young bachelor can retire to his apartment without much concern that anything he does behind closed doors will be witnessed. His ancestors could not enjoy such privacy. The question that is now emerging, however, is whether the private life of this bachelor *can* be kept from others' scrutiny. For although it may be possible to keep others from directly observing our "private" actions, it may not be possible to avoid their indirect scrutiny. The young bachelor may engage in illegal drug use in private, but his actions are *knowable* through the use of drug tests.

Similarly, the individual who is infected with the HIV virus may have contracted it in the course of "private" pursuits (e.g., sexual relations with an infected partner). There is much that takes place behind closed doors that has significant implications for others.

I distinguished earlier between those things that are *legitimately* safe-guarded from others' scrutiny (i.e., private acts) and those that are il-legitimately hidden (i.e., secret acts). The distinction between privacy and secrecy is negotiable and changes over time. Things once viewed as secret are occasionally redefined as private, and vice-versa. As this happens, the distinction between private and public becomes less clear. Are young people's sexual behaviors private? In one sense they are. The young bachelor is entitled to engage in consensual heterosexual sex in the privacy of his apartment (in most states). But if others demand evidence about the consequences of those behaviors, it becomes less clear whether they are public or private. The distinction becomes blurred. That may be why many view the proliferation of computerized banks of personal information and the use of ordeals as having caused a loss of privacy.

To the extent that privacy is perceived to permit activities that threaten others, the boundary between secrecy and privacy may shift subtly. This is precisely what is now happening with respect to "unsafe" sexual behaviors. Due to the potential consequences of sexual activities that take place in private, there is increasing pressure to know about them. We are still entitled to our privacy in sexual matters *so long as* we do not engage in "unsafe" (i.e., illegitimate) practices that might threaten others. But how can we know whether someone has engaged in such dangerous behaviors? Thirty years ago it may have been possible to have sexual relations with little fear of the consequences (except the possibility of pregnancy). That is no longer true. It is no longer possible to *trust* a sexual partner who is not well known. It is such a lack of trust that leads to greater surveillance because surveillance may permit us to trust others. The partner who presents the results of an HIV test can be trusted (with respect to the threat of transmitting the virus). Has there been a loss of privacy with respect to sexual behaviors as a result of the threat of AIDS? Perhaps there has.

The perspective developed in this book, however, suggests another interpretation. When portable reputations are seen as an alternative to more conventional ways of knowing another person, or when they are seen as a consequence of others' anonymity, they may be interpreted as the costs we accept as part of that anonymity.

Such costs are neither inherently good nor bad. Instead, they are aspects of a complex society in which vast numbers of unacquainted individuals must be able to depend on one another. Our willingness to accept these costs depends on how much they contribute to the maintenance of trust, the irreducible minimum requirement for sustained human interaction. Trust is the core around which all communities and societies are built. Surveillance may sustain or permit it in a complex society. The costs of privacy are then seen as the costs of trust.

APPENDICES

Appendix A. All Series Used in Graphs
(See Graphs for Sources)

YEAR	MMA2024	MMA2529	MFE2024	MFE2529	MNOT	FNOT	MNOT2	FNOT2
1947	5653	5540	6095	6014	3.17	3.00	2.64	2.13
1948	5763	5589	6047	5933	5.10	5.11	4.88	7.94
1949	5591	5598	5952	5991	4.44	3.29	5.31	4.34
1950	5544	5733	5863	6039	5.56	6.16	4.80	3.92
1951	4964	5706	5766	6210	7.23	7.21	4.50	4.51
1952	4240	6754	5656	6188	4.88	5.85	5.05	3.89
1954	3902	5570	5412	6045	8.51	6.91	7.50	4.30
1955	3978	5602	5386	5952	4.90	7.58	8.28	4.52
1956	4260	5565	5345	5864	6.67	6.19	8.41	3.70
1957	4419	5472	5324	5788	7.20	7.08	7.04	4.37
1958	4666	5424	5398	5676	7.93	6.84	8.46	5.11
1959	4757	5378	5485	5561	7.86	7.35	8.78	4.48
1960	4961	5309	5591	5518	7.30	7.44	7.67	3.97
1961	5084	5304	5720	5498	8.44	7.90	9.39	4.97
1962	5096	5162	5869	5484	8.59	7.84	9.45	5.43
1963	5461	5214	6154	5525	7.69	7.17	8.73	4.58
1964	5810	5229	6445	5586	7.01	7.28	6.73	4.67
1965	6074	5351	6702	5678	8.53	8.00	8.37	4.16
1966	5969	5411	6905	5788	8.38	7.08	8.19	4.89
1967	6226	5642	7340	5992	9.30	7.00	8.17	5.24
1968	6594	6027	7707	6323	7.55	8.33	7.65	4.48
1969	6753	6341	8040	6608	9.42	8.10	8.41	5.43
1970	7206	6659	8386	6854	9.03	8.04	8.73	5.76
1971	7837	6866	8757	7049	10.21	9.52	10.37	6.33

Year	MMA2024	MMA2529	MFE2024	MFE2529				
1972	8247	7117	8992	7361	12.79	9.06	10.45	7.25
1973	8507	7483	9114	7737	12.87	9.96	12.32	6.80
1974	8648	7724	9193	8008	15.38	11.36	14.44	8.09
1975	8995	8048	9406	8345	15.53	10.72	14.92	8.40
1976	9197	8465	9614	8754	16.17	12.94	16.57	10.27
1977	9426	8592	9804	8868	17.91	14.08	18.10	11.65
1978	9572	8650	9989	8953	19.53	15.84	20.40	12.42
1979	9713	8812	10136	9128	20.81	16.99	21.74	13.34
1980	9801	9076	10246	9357	21.48	16.46	23.16	14.47
1981	10300	9713	10685	9978	21.08	16.53	23.99	14.95
1982	10363	9968	10716	10224	19.86	16.38	23.95	15.71
1983	10379	10221	10682	10416	18.23	16.00	24.61	15.19
1984	10388	10443	10620	10603	18.82	16.04	24.32	14.84
1985	10055	10420	10411	10686	21.20	16.42	25.37	15.21
1986	9788	10751	10160	10868	21.48	17.92	26.32	16.54
1987	9499	10694	9859	10942	20.94	17.54	25.36	16.03
1988	9254	10669	9586	10854	21.83	17.90	26.22	16.82
1989	8939	10650	9336	10827	22.81	19.74	27.47	17.39
1990	8811	10515	9177	10685	24.02	19.28	26.87	18.18
1991	8839	10331	9148	10436	22.48	18.54	27.91	17.59

Definitions:
MMA2024 = Males 20–24 (Thousands), MMA2529 = Males 25–29, MFE2024 = Females 20–24,
MFE2529 = Females 25–29, MNOT = % Males 20–24 not in families, FNOT = % Females 20–24 not in
families, MNOT2 = % Males 25–29 not in families, FNOT2 = % Females 25–29 not in families,
MA2024DL = % Males 20–24 with drivers licenses, FE2024DL = % Females 20–24 with drivers licenses,
MA2529CO = % Males 25–29 with at least 4 years of college, FE2529CO = % of Females 25–29 with at
least 4 years of college, MFCREDT = % males and females under 25 with bank credit cards,
DRUGTST = % employers who require preemployment drug tests, PSYCHTST = % of employer who
require preemployment psychological tests.

Appendix B

YEAR	MA2024DL	FE2024DL	MA2529CO	FE2529CO	MFCREDT	DRUGTST	PSYCHTST
1947	—	—	5.80	5.40	—	—	—
1948	—	—	7.93	3.56	—	—	—
1949	—	—	8.50	4.04	—	—	—
1950	—	—	9.60	5.90	—	—	—
1951	—	—	9.66	5.00	—	—	—
1952	—	—	13.80	6.70	—	—	—
1954	—	—	11.39	6.44	—	—	—
1955	—	—	11.97	6.92	—	—	—
1956	—	—	12.55	7.40	—	—	—
1957	—	—	13.50	7.50	—	—	—
1958	—	—	13.70	8.36	—	—	—
1959	—	—	14.80	7.60	—	—	—
1960	—	—	14.86	9.32	—	—	—
1961	—	—	15.43	9.80	—	—	—
1962	—	—	17.20	9.20	—	—	—
1963	96.20	69.40	16.59	10.75	—	—	—
1964	94.80	71.20	16.60	9.20	—	—	—
1965	95.60	73.50	15.60	9.50	—	—	—
1966	96.00	73.50	16.80	11.30	—	—	—
1967	92.70	73.20	17.20	12.10	—	—	—
1968	91.80	73.60	18.00	11.60	—	—	—
1969	91.90	75.40	19.40	12.80	—	—	—
1970	92.80	78.10	20.00	12.90	12.00	—	—
1971	91.30	76.80	20.10	13.80	—	—	—
1972	93.90	80.70	22.00	16.00	—	—	—

Year							
1973	93.00	81.10	21.60	16.40	—	—	—
1974	94.00	83.30	23.90	17.60	—	—	—
1975	95.20	85.30	25.10	18.70	—	—	—
1976	95.80	85.80	27.50	20.10	—	—	12.00
1977	96.00	86.30	27.00	21.10	18.00	—	17.00
1978	94.30	85.50	26.00	20.60	—	—	—
1979	93.20	85.00	25.60	20.50	—	—	—
1980	91.90	84.40	24.10	20.90	—	—	14.00
1981	91.10	83.50	23.10	19.60	—	—	—
1982	92.20	85.80	23.30	20.20	—	—	—
1983	95.40	88.40	23.90	21.10	20.00	—	—
1984	91.70	85.20	23.20	20.70	22.00	16.00	30.00
1985	91.50	85.10	23.10	21.30	24.80	6.00	21.00
1986	92.20	84.60	22.90	21.90	25.00	16.00	30.00
1987	93.20	85.30	22.30	21.70	32.30	21.00	28.00
1988	92.20	84.60	23.20	21.80	31.20	27.00	—
1989	92.70	86.40	23.80	22.80	34.20	32.00	30.00
1990	92.40	86.50	23.70	22.80	—	47.00	32.00
1991	—	—	23.00	23.40	—	—	—

Definitions:

MMA2024 = Males 20–24 (Thousands), MMA2529 = Males 25–29, MFE2024 = Females 20–24,
MFE2529 = Females 25–29, MNOT = % Males 20–24 not in families, FNOT = % Females 20–24 not in
families, MNOT2 = % Males 25–29 not in families, FNOT2 = % Females 25–29 not in families,
MA2024DL = % Males 20–24 with drivers licenses, FE2024DL = % Females 20–24 with drivers licenses,
MA2529CO = % Males 25–29 with at least 4 years of college, FE2529CO = % of Females 25–29 with at
least 4 years of college, MFCREDT = % males and females under 25 with bank credit cards,
DRUGTST = % employers who require preemployment drug tests, PSYCHTST = % of employer who
require preemployment psychological tests.

REFERENCES

Ackerman, Deborah L. 1991. "A History of Drug Testing." Pp. 1–21 in R. H. Coombs and L. J. West (eds.), *Drug Testing: Issues and Options*. New York: Oxford University Press.

Aldhous, Peter. 1991. "Closing a Loophole in Discrimination Rules." *Nature* 351:684.

American Medical Association 1990. "Genetic Screening by Employers." Office of the General Council. *Journal of the American Medical Association* (7), 1005–1008.

Bacon, Margaret K., Herbert Barry, III, and Irvin L. Child. 1952. "Rater's Instructions for Analysis of Socialization Practices with Respect to Dependence and Independence." Mimeographed. Cited in Roberts (1965).

Bailey, Beth L. 1988. *From Front Porch to Back Seat: Courtship in Twentieth-Century America*. Baltimore: Johns Hopkins University Press.

Barland, Gordon H. 1988. "The Polygraph Test in the U.S.A. and Elsewhere." Pp. 73–95 in Anthony Gale (ed.), *The Polygraph Test: Lies, Truth and Science*, Chapter 7. London: Sage Publications.

Barrett, Paul. 1983. *The Automobile and Urban Transit: The Formation of Public Policy in Chicago, 1900–1930*. Philadelphia: Temple University Press.

Bartlett, Robert. 1986. *Trial by Fire and Water: The Medieval Judicial Ordeal*. Oxford: Clarendon Press.

Board of Governors of the Federal Reserve System. 1949. Survey of Consumer Finances. Federal Reserve Bulletin, 35.

———. 1957. *Consumer Installment Credit*. Washington, D.C.: U.S. Government Printing Office.

Briggs, Jean. 1970. *Never in Anger: Portrait of an Eskimo Family*. Cambridge, MA: Harvard University Press.

Brown, Peter. 1982. "Society and the Supernatural: A Medieval Change." Reprinted in *Society and the Holy in Late Antiquity* by Peter Brown. 1982. Berkeley: University of California Press.

Burr, George L. (ed.). 1914. *Narratives of the Witchcraft Cases, 1648–1706*. New York: Charles Scribner's.

Canner, Glen. 1987. "Changes in Consumer Holding and Use of Credit Cards, 1970–86." *Journal of Retail Banking* 18:13–24.

Coleman, James S. 1971. *The Adolescent Society: The Social Life of the Teenager and Its Impact on Education.* New York: Free Press.

Collins, Randall. 1979. *The Credential Society: A Historical Sociology of Education and Stratification.* New York: Academic Press.

Committee on Government Operations. 1988. "Failing the Test: Proficiency Standards Are Needed for Drug Testing Laboratories." Thirty-third report by the Committee on Government Operations, 100th Congress, 2nd session, House report 100-527.

Coombs, Robert L., and Louis Jolyon West. 1991. *Drug Testing: Issues and Options.* New York: Oxford University Press.

Decresce, Robert P., Mark S. Lifshitz, John Ambre, Adrianne Mazura, Joseph Tilson, and Kathryn Cochran. 1989. *Drug Testing in the Workplace..* Chicago: ASCP Press.

Department of Health and Human Services. 1988. *Mandatory Guidelines for Federal Workplace Drug Testing Programs.* Federal Regulation 11,970.

Douglas, James A., Daniel E. Feld, and Nancy Asquith. 1989. *Employment Testing Manual.* Boston: Warren, Gorham & Lamont.

Elkin, Frederick and Gerald Handel 1984. *The Child and Society: The Process of Socialization,* 4th ed. New York: Random House.

Federal Bureau of Investigation (FBI). 1980. "The Polygraph Technique: Past and Present." Reprinted from the FBI Law Enforcement Bulletin, June 1980.

Flaherty, David H. 1972. *Privacy in Colonial New England.* Charlottesville, VA: University of Virginia Press.

Flink, James J. 1970. *America Adopts the Automobile, 1895–1910.* Cambridge, MA: MIT Press

Friedman, Scott E. 1992. *The Law of Parent-Child Relationships.* Chicago: American Bar Association.

Goldscheider, Calvin, and Frances K. Goldscheider. 1987. "Moving Out and Marriage: What Do Young Adults Expect?" *American Sociological Review* 52 (April):278–285.

Goldscheider, Frances K., and Julie DaVanzo. 1989. "Pathways to Independent Living in Early Adulthood: Marriage, Semiautonomy, and Premarital Residential Independence." *Demography* 26 (4):597–614.

Goldscheider, Frances K., and Celine LeBourdais. 1986. "The Decline in Age at Leaving Home 1920–1979." *Sociology and Social Research* 70 (January):143–145.

Hayge, Harold 1989. Survey of Employer Anti-Drug Programs. U.S. Department of Labor. Bureau of Labor Statistics. Report 760.

————. 1991. "Anti-Drug programs in the Workplace: Are They Here to Stay?" *Monthly Labor Review* (April):26–29.

Halpern, Sue. 1992. *Migrations to Solitude.* New York: Pantheon Books.

Hechter, Michael. 1987. *Principles of Group Solidarity.* Berkeley: University of California Press.

Heller, Agnes. 1985. *The Power of Shame: A Rational Perspective.* Boston: Routledge and Kegan Paul.

Hirschman, Elizabeth, Mark Alpert, and Rajendra Strivastava. 1980. "Consumer Credit Card Usage and Retail Purchasing." *Journal of Retail Banking* 2(1) (March):54–66.

Hollinger, Richard C., and John P. Clark. 1983. *Theft by Employees.* Lexington, MA: Lexington Books.

Huggins, Marlene, Maurice Bloch, Shelin Kanani, Oliver Quarrell, Jane Theilman, Amy Hedrick, Bernard Dickens, Abbyann Lynch, and Michael Hayden. 1990. "Ethical and Legal dilemmas Arising during Predictive Testing for Adult-Onset Disease: The Experience of Huntington Disease." *American Journal of Human Genetics* 47:4–12.

Jones, John W., and William Terris. 1991. "Selection Alternatives to the Preemployment Polygraph." Pp. 39–52 in J. W. Jones (ed.), *Preemployment Honesty Testing: Current Research and Future Directions,* Chapter 3. New York: Quorum Books.

Katz, Sanford N., William A. Schroeder, and Lawrence R. Sidman. 1973. "Emancipating our Children—Coming of Legal Age in America." *Family Law Quarterly* VII(3): 211–241.

Kett, Joseph F. 1977. *Rites of Passage: Adolescence in America, 1790 to the Present.* New York: Basic Books.

Krygier, Martin. 1983. "Publicness, Privateness, and 'Primitive Law.'" Pp. 307–340 in Stanley I. Benn and Gerald F. Gaus (eds.), *Public and Private in Social Life.* London: St. Martin's Press.

Larson, John A. 1938. "The Lie Detector Polygraph: Its History and Development." *Journal of the Michigan State Medical Society* 37:893–897.

Lea, Henry Charles. 1973. In Edward Peters (ed.), *The Ordeal.* Philadelphia: University of Pennsylvania Press (originally published in 1866 as *Part III, Superstition and Force*).

Lo, Bernard. 1991. "Ethical Issues in Drug Testing." Pp. 190–201 in Robert H. Coombs and Louis J. West (eds.), *Drug Testing: Issues and Options,* Chapter 9. New York: Oxford University Press.

Lombroso, Cesare. 1895. *L'Homme Criminel.* Paris: Felix Alcan.

Lykken, David Thoreson. 1981. *A Tremor in the Blood: Uses and Abuses of the Lie Detector.* New York: McGraw Hill.

Mandell, Lewis. 1990. *The Credit Card Industry: A History.* Boston: Twayne Publishers.

Marston, William M. 1938. *The Lie Detector Test.* New York: Richard R. Smith.

Mediamark Research, Inc. 1990. *Banking, Investments, and Credit Cards Report: Spring, 1989.* Series P-6.

Michigan State University: Career Development and Placement Services. 1991. *Recruiting Trends: 1990–1991* (and other years as noted).

Miike, Lawrence. 1987. Testimony before the Senate Committee on the Judiciary, April 9, 1987 "Accuracy and Reliability of Urine Drug Tests." In "Proficiency Standards for Drug Testing Laboratories," Hearings before a subcommittee of the Committee on Government Operations, House of Representatives, 100th Congress, June 10 and 11, 1987.

Mizruchi, Ephraim H. 1983. *Regulating Society: Marginality and Social Control in Historical Perspective.* New York: Free Press.

Modell, John. 1989. *Into One's Own: From Youth to Adulthood in the United States, 1920–1975.* Berkeley, CA: University of California Press.

Moore, Barrington, Jr. 1984. *Privacy: Studies in Social and Cultural History.* Armonk, NY: M.E. Sharpe.

National Institute on Drug Abuse. 1991. "National Household Survey on Drug Abuse: Highlights 1990."

National Institute of Mental Health. 1989. *Approaching the 21st Century: Opportunities for NIMH Neuroscience Research.* Rockville, MD: U.S. Department of Health and Human Services, NIMH (ADM) 88–1580.

———. 1990. "Statement from the National Institutes of Health Workshop on Population Screening for the Cystic Fibrosis Gene." *New England Journal of Medicine* 323(1):70–71.

Nelkin, Dorothy and Laurence Tancredi. 1989. *Dangerous Diagnoses.* New York: Basic Books.

Nock, Steven L., and Paul W. Kingston. 1990. *The Sociology of Public Issues.* Belmont, CA: Wadsworth.

Orentlicher, David 1990. "Genetic Screening by Employers." Journal of the American Medical Association 263 (February): 1005–1008.

Parsons, Talcott. 1959. "The School Class as a Social System: Some of Its Functions in American Society." *Harvard Educational Review* 29:297–318.

———. 1971. "Kinship and the Associational Aspect of Social Structure." Pp. 409–438 in F. L. K. Hsu (ed.) *Kinship and Culture.* Chicago: Aldine.

Popenoe, David. 1985. *Private Pleasure, Public Plight.* New Brunswick, NJ: Transaction Books.

Posner, Richard A. 1981. *The Economics of Justice.* Cambridge, MA: Harvard University Press.

Radding, Charles M. 1989. "Superstition to Science: Nature, Fortune, and the Passing of the Medieval Ordeal." *American Historical Review* 84(4) (October):945–969.

Roberts, John M. 1965 "Oaths, Autonomic Ordeals, and Power." *American Anthropologist* 67(6) (part 2) (December):186–212.

Sackett, Paul R., Laura R. Burris, and Chirstine Callahan. 1989. "Integrity Testing for Personnel Selection: An Update." *Personnel Psychology,* 42 (Autumn):491–529.

Sennett, Richard. 1978. *The Fall of Public Man.* New York: Random House.

Shils, Edward. 1966. "Privacy: Its Constitution and Vicissitudes." *Law and Contemporary Problems* 31 (Spring):281–306.

Sikorski, Hon. Gerry 1988. Joint Hearing before the Subcommittee on Human Resources and Subcommittee on Civil Service. House of Representatives. Oversight Hearing on Administration Plans to Drug Test Federal Work Force, Thursday, June 16, 1988.

Simmel, Georg. 1908. Soziologie, Untersuchungen uber die Former der Vergesellschaftung. In Kurt H. Wolff (trans. and ed.), *The Sociology of Georg Simmel,* 1950. New York: Free Press.

Taylor, Gabriele. 1985. *Pride, Shame, and Guilt: Emotions of Self Assessment.* New York: Oxford University Press.

Trovillo, Paul V. 1939. "A History of Lie Detection," 29(6) (March–April):848–881, continued in 30(1):104–119.

Turner, Ralph H. 1960. "Sponsored and Contest Mobility and the School System." *American Socioological Review* 25:855–867.

U.S. Bureau of the Census. 1975. *Historical Statistics of the United States: Colonial Times to the Present.* Washington, D.C.: U.S. Government Printing Office.

———. 1979. *Marital Status and Living Arrangements: March, 1978.* Washington, D.C.: CPR Series P-20, No. 338. U.S. Government Printing Office.

———. 1990. *Studies in Household and Family Formation.* CPR, Series P-23: No. 169. Washington, D.C.: U.S. Government Printing Office.

———. 1991a. *Marital Status and Living Arrangements: March, 1990.* CPR Series P-20, No. 450. Washington, D.C.: U.S. Government Printing Office.

———. 1991b. *Statistical Abstract of the United States: 1990.* Washington, D.C.: U.S. Government Printing Office.

———. 1992. *Household and Family Characteristics: March, 1991.* CPR Series P-20, No. 458. Washington, D.C.: U.S. Government Printing Office.

U.S. Congress, Office of Technology Assessment. 1983. *Scientific Validity of Polygraph Testing.* Washington, D.C.: U.S. Government Printing Office.

———. 1989. *Genetic Monitoring and Screening in the Workplace.* OTA-BA-455. Washington, D.C.: U.S. Government Printing Office.

————. 1990a. "The Use of Integrity Tests for Pre-Employment Screening." OTA-SET-442. Washington, D.C.: U.S. Government Printing Office.

————. 1990b. *Genetic Witness: Forensic Uses of DNA Tests*. Washington, D.C.: U.S. Government Printing Office.

U.S. Department of Health and Human Services. 1981. *The legal Status of Adolescents 1980*. Washington, D.C.: U.S. Government Printing Office.

U.S. Department of Labor, Women's Bureau. 1969. *Handbook on Women Workers*. Bulletin No. 294. Washington, D.C.: U.S. Government Printing Office.

U.S. Department of Transportation, Federal Highway Administration. 1977. *Highway Statistics: Summary to 1975*. Washington, D.C.: U.S. Government Printing Office.

————. 1991. *Highway Statistics: 1989*. Washington, D.C.: U.S. Government Printing Office.

U.S. Department of Transportation, National Highway Traffic Safety Administration. 1980. *Driver Licensing Laws Annotated*. Washington, D.C.: U.S. Government Printing Office.

————. 1982. *Driver Licensing Laws Annotated*. Washington, D.C.: U.S. Government Printing Office.

U.S. Senate. 1987. *Polygraph Protection Act of 1987*. February 2, 1987. 100th Congress, Senate report 100–284.

————. 1988. "Developments in Drug and Alcohol Testing." Hearing before Committee on Commerce, Science, and Transportation. U.S. Senate, February 25, 1988.

Veblin, Thorstein. 1961. "The Theory of the Leisure Class." In T. Parsons, E. Shils, K. Naegele, and J. Pitts (eds.), *Theories of Society*. New York: The Free Press.

Waite, Linda J., Frances K. Goldscheider, and Christina Witsberger. 1986. "Nonfamily Living and the Erosion of Traditional Family Orientations Among Young Adults." *American Sociological Review* 51 (August):541–554.

Waller, Willard. 1938. *The Family: A Dynamic Interpretation*. New York: The Cordon Company.

Warren, Carol, and Barbara Laslett. 1977. "Privacy and Secrecy: A Conceptual Comparison." *Journal of Social Issues* 33:43–51.

Weber, Max. 1958. "The Protestant Sects and the Spirit of Capitalism." Pp. 302–322 in Hans Gerth and C. Wright Mills (eds.), *From Max Weber: Essays in Sociology*. New York: Oxford University Press.

Werner, Steven H., Dennis S. Joy, and John W. Jones. 1991. "Improving Corporate Profitability with Preemployment Integrity Tests." Pp. 53–61 in J.W. Jones (ed.), *Preemployment Honesty Testing: Current Research and Future Directions*, Chapter 4. New York: Quorum Books.

INDEX

Ordeals *(continued)*
  hot iron, 77–78, 90
  knowledge gained by, 126
  limitations of, 109
  in medieval times, 75, 79–80
  in modern America, 76, 84
  oath and, 79
  purpose of, 74, 81–82
  replacements of, 80–81
  reputations and, 3, 76–77
  sex crimes and, 78
  societies relying on, 83–84
  strangers and, 76
  surveillance and, as form of, 76, 83
  in thirteenth century, 80
  trust and, 76–77
  in twelfth century, 80
  validity and, 82–83
  in workplace, 92

Paternity tests, 128
Peer culture, 31–32, 37
Plethysmograph, 85
Polygraph, 86, 88 *(See also* Lie detector
    test)
Polygraph Protection Act, 91
Preemployment screening
  drug testing in, 107–108
  integrity testing in, 92, 93–94, 97
Premarital relationships, 32, 37
Privacy
  absence of widespread, 43
  in ancient Hebrew culture, 10
  changes in, 109
  in Colonial New England, 10
  costs of, 1, 11, 130–131
  cross-cultural analysis of, 10
  definition of, 12
  in modern America, 1, 11–13
  sexual, 63–64
  sharing of, 12
  unknown information and, 110
  in Utku society, 9–10
  violation of, 12, 13
Psychological personality inventories,
    94

Relationships, human, 110–111
Reputations *(See also* Genetic and bio-
    chemical reputations)
  bad, 2, 3

credentials and, 3
drivers' licenses and, 58
drug testing and, 98
educational degrees and, 69–70
family name and, 4, 126
good, 2–3
importance of, 124–125
industrialization and, 49–50
ordeals and, 3, 76–77
portable, 69–70, 127
privacy and, 111–112
reliable and predictive, 127
sketchiness of, 109
strangers and, 10
surveillance and, 44
traditional maintenance of, 46–48
trust and, 2–3
Responsibility, 83–84
Ripurian Law, 77
Rituals, 14, 15, 76 *(See also* Ordeals)
Rounds Brothers v. McDaniel (1909), 21

Salic Law, 77
Schools, 65–66, 119–121 *(See also* Edu-
    cational degrees)
Secrecy, 8, 130
Secularization, 47
Shame, 7, 8, 65, 84
Social class, 4, 67
Social control, 16, 38, 41, 65
Socialization, 4
Social order, 1–2
Solitary living
  effect of, 12–13
  emancipated youths and, 5–6, 18,
    85
Sorcery, 81
Sphygmomanometer, 88, 89
Sponsored mobility system, 66
Standardized tests, 119
Statistical norms, 113
Strangers
  credentials and, 43
  emancipated youths as, 23
  lies and, 73
  ordeals and, 76
  privacy and, 1, 9–10, 11, 14
  reputations and, 10
  surveillance and, 3, 46
  trust and, 1, 3
Supervision *(See* Surveillance)